The Missouri Review

Volume XIV Number 2 1991

University of Missouri-Columbia

The Missouri Review is published by the College of Arts & Science of the University of Missouri-Columbia, with private contributions and assistance from the Missouri Arts Council and the National Endowment for the Arts.

The diary of Jean L. Clemens is by arrangement with the Huntington Library.

The photographs of Jean Clemens (1892-1900 #3 and 1892-1909 #7) courtesy of the Mark Twain Memorial, Hartford, CT.

Cartoons in this issue by Marian Henley.

The editors invite submissions of poetry, fiction, and essays of a general literary interest with a distinctly contemporary orientation. Manuscripts will not be returned unless accompanied by a stamped, self-addressed envelope. Please address all correspondence to The Editors, The Missouri Review, 1507 Hillcrest Hall, University of Missouri, Columbia, Missouri 65211.

SUBSCRIPTIONS

1 year (3 issues), $12.00
2 years (6 issues), $21.00
3 years (9 issues), $30.00

Copyright © 1991 by The Curators of the University of Missouri
ISSN 0191 1961
ISBN 1-879758-01-6

Typesetting by HiTec Typeset, Columbia, MO.
Printed by Thomson-Shore, Dexter, MI.

The Missouri Review

CONTENTS

1991

ESSAYS

Marian Henley creates "Maxine," the syndicated weekly comic strip. She is also the author of a cartoon novel by the same title.

Foreword

Many of the contributors to this issue are travellers. Their journeys may take them a modest distance or a long way, to destinations exotic or commonplace, desirable or less than desirable. Some of their journeys are not taken entirely by choice. All of them, though, are full of discoveries.

Among the short stories, Ursula Le Guin's protagonist in "Geezers" embarks only on a weekend getaway, but while making this brief jaunt, realizes he is facing a whole new world. Kate Wheeler's adolescent hero in "Improving My Average" is always moving from one faraway place to another—now to Cartagena, Colombia, where she is about to learn one of the terrible lessons of growing up. A businessman in Kevin McDermott's superb story "Magic and Hidden Things" travels to Port-au-Prince, Haiti, a trip he doesn't at all relish. We are proud to note, by the way, that this is Mr. McDermott's first short story published in the U.S.

Peter Ford's "Around the Edge," from his upcoming book, describes an expedition he took in 1988 around the Caribbean coast of South America; in this episode Ford recounts his passage from Honduras to Nicaragua and down the Coco River in the company of Indian guerillas. Travel for Judith Ortiz Cofer becomes partly an act of personal liberation. A third essay, "Lily My Sweet" by Judy Ruiz, is a beautiful and frightening portrayal of a sojourn in a state mental institution.

In our interview, novelist Thomas Sanchez describes a restless and obsessive creative life. While writing *Rabbit Boss* Sanchez had to leave this country and live and write in Spain—getting away from a place in order to understand it—a type of experience that is surprisingly common in creative endeavors. Sanchez is one of the more interesting novelists today, applying his considerable talents to ideas, movements, large thematic and even public concerns, as well as to character.

This issue's poets are all travellers, ranging freely and often using faraway locations for their settings. Miniaturists and stay-at-homes they are not. David Wojahn travels through history as well as to foreign locales in these offerings from his upcoming collection *Late Empire*. James Solheim is widely published but has not yet done a book—a whimsical writer who creates a world too fantastic and fully imagined to discredit. Roger Weingarten includes significant new poems from his next collection, among them its title work "Jungle

Gliders." Walter Bargen is known primarily as a poet of nature, but these new poems demonstrate wider interests and subjects from the American inner city to a magical visit to Costa Rica.

Fans of Mark Twain will recall that Twain was out of this country on a nearly decade-long journey to Europe after his business and financial failures during the 1880s. For his family—especially his two daughters—coming back to the United States was like going to a foreign land. Jean Clemens, the younger daughter, began her diary during this time, and it is intriguing in many ways—for the images that it gives us of New York in the year 1900, for a peek at family life during the climax of the Victorian era, and for the first-hand account it affords of a young woman who has sometimes been characterized by her father's biographers—wrongly, I believe—as a rather pitiful victim. As a young woman who had a severe and persistent form of epilepsy before the age of effective treatments, Jean Clemens was courageous in her attitude towards her condition.

SM

MAGIC AND HIDDEN THINGS
/ Kevin McDermott

T HE PART OF HIS JOB Creech used to like least was having
to visit Port-au-Prince. Four hours from New York, it may
as well have been the dark side of the moon. Approaching the
airport the plane would cruise low along the coast, over the pale
eroded mountains and silted rivers. The jungle that once covered
the country was nearly all gone. A few palm trees waved and
nodded on the fringe around the runway of the airport, and above
a nearby cluster of small cinderblock houses painted pink and
lavender.

Creech's last trip was in June, 1987, after the Duvaliers had
been tossed out. The army junta running the country seemed, to
general amazement, about to deliver on a promise of elections.
This was good news for Creech's interests in Port-au-Prince, where
his firm sorted several million supermarket coupons a year in a
plant leased from a man named Henry Bajeux. Costs were low
in Haiti and the short flight time was convenient, but Bajeux had
been shut down repeatedly by strikes. Haiti might still make sense
if the labor situation stabilized, but if the strikes continued Creech
was going to recommend taking the coupons to Mexico before the
end of summer.

When his plane landed Creech rented a white Ford. The road from
the airport to the city went past the barnlike assembly plants where
Haiti's only resource—cheap labor—made underwear, baseballs and
low-tech gadgets. The road went right past Bajeux's place. Outside
his gate a woman had set up shop on a pair of packing crates; she
was selling mangoes and bundles of charcoal. She wore a scarf
on her head in the brutal sun and her black skirt was tugged
modestly over her knees. She was waiting patiently for someone
in a car to stop; there were any number of people passing on
foot, but they surely had no money to buy. A yard or two from
where she sat a grey donkey stood tethered to Bajeux's fence,
looking rather unsteady on its legs. It made Creech think of a
drunken man.

Creech always stayed at the St. Charles, up in the salubrious
hills above Port-au-Prince, not quite as far up as Petionville. The St.
Charles was on a quiet street of comfortable private homes, many

in the pretty gingerbread style featured in travel brochures. There was no obvious place to leave his car so Creech simply parked in the gravel drive in front of the hotel; a flashy Mitsubishi jeep was already there ahead of him. A smiling young man appeared from somewhere and immediately reached for his bags. He spoke English and introduced himself as Roger. Roger claimed to be the bellboy. Creech knew that was a lie, but he let him take the bags inside. His suspicions were confirmed in the hostile way in which Mme. St. Charles stared at the kid as they came in. Roger was cowed before her tough gaze, and when Creech slipped him a dollar he dematerialized as abruptly as he had appeared.

"*Bonjour, madame*," said Creech. "Do you remember me? Mr. Creech?"

"*Bienvenu*, Monsieur Creech. Good seeing you again. Have a good trip?"

"Very nice. Were you able to save me a corner room?" There was a chance of having a breeze at night in a corner room.

"You will be comfortable. Edouard," said Mme. St. Charles, calling to her son. He was in a small office working at a ledger. "Help Mr. Creech." Edouard did as he was told and lugged the bags up three flights of stairs to the room. Creech gave another dollar to him.

Rooms at the St. Charles were spare. Two single beds at right angles to each other, a pipe for hanging clothes, a three-drawer bureau. On the bureau was an oscillating fan and a thermos of ice water. The hotel claimed the water was bottled, but Creech would not drink it; pale particles of something suspended in it made him think of human skin or dissolved feces. He unpacked three bottles of Evian he'd brought down with him, and when he showered he was careful not to swallow. In Haiti Creech was a compulsive showerer, a real American. He always felt dusty and sweaty, which indeed he always was. He showered before dinner, sharing the stall with a pale-green lizard that would not move when his eye was on it, but which in the instant he blinked could cover six inches.

Before dinner Creech walked out on the wide roof terrace to look over the city and get a breath of air. A breeze tossed the tops of the palms about, which grew taller than the third floor of the hotel. The breeze carried the breath of the city up from the bottom of the hill, human scents and always somewhere the aroma of charcoal burning. Down there people were cooking whatever they cooked for dinner, swatting their kids, talking on corners, making love on blankets, pissing in the mud or in the street by the curbside. Down there it was night, but out on the ocean, in the direction of Jamaica, the sun was still above the horizon, throwing a splendid orange light full across the water of the claw-shaped harbor. A freight ship with a single bow light was moving out across this lighted path toward the sea.

"Good evening."

Creech had not seen the woman on the other side of the terrace. She spoke to him from a chaise longue where she sat reading a newspaper; it was not an American paper or one of the Haitian papers he knew. Creech said, "Hi. It's a terrific view from up here, isn't it?" He was feeling social.

"Yes," said the woman. "Pretty."

She was a white woman, a bit on the stout side and very fair; she could not have been in Haiti very long. She folded her newspaper in her lap. "Do you have an idea of when dinner is served?" she asked.

"About six," he told her. From the open windows beneath them he heard the conversation of the staff and the clank of silverware and plates being laid on tables.

"I am suddenly hungry," said the woman. "I have been sitting here quite contentedly reading and drowsing, but I am suddenly hungry. You were on the plane coming down from New York this afternoon. I walked behind you when we arrived. I recognize you."

The plane had not been too full on the way down, and Creech was surprised that he had not seen her. He asked what brought her to Haiti; a Westerner in Port-au-Prince always had a more interesting reason for being there than pleasure. Even from the little she said Creech heard some kind of hard German touch in her English.

"For a sort of jamboree, I suppose you would call it. I am a Sister of St. Ursula. My hospital is in the Philippines, but every two years we meet to compare our work. This year we are in Port-au-Prince. Perhaps you know our clinic in Cité Soleil?"

"You're a nun," said Creech. "A sister."

"You've got it."

The sister asked him what his business was, and once she got started she was a whirlwind of questions. She seemed especially interested in knowing if Creech were married. When he said he was she wanted to know for how many years, how old his children were, how his wife coped when he was away.

"I'm a nosey biddy," she admitted, pronouncing the double *d* hard in "biddy," not like an American would do. "I hope you don't mind so many questions." He didn't mind; she was genial about it, and anyway Creech missed his family when he traveled and was glad to talk. She said her name was Margaret Kriemhild, but people, she said, called her Meta. Meta said she was from Liechtenstein.

They had dinner together on the open porch downstairs. Street-noise—children yelling and automobiles downshifting as they went up the steep hill past the hotel and drums somewhere—carried over the stone wall that surrounded the property. Every dinner at the St. Charles included a huge pile of boiled rice pilaf, and that night there was also oxtail soup and broiled chicken. "Mealtimes are comforting when one is traveling," Meta observed, digging in with enthusiasm. Creech agreed, but added that in Haiti he never enjoyed a meal without being conscious of receiving more nourishment in one sitting than someone living just over the stone wall might get in a week. It was guilt inducing, he told her.

"Yes," said Meta, "but short of taking your own plate out to the street and giving it to the first beggar you see, what will you do? Eh? Hunger is complex," she said, "and feeling guilty doesn't make a dent. We must always be grateful for our good luck."

Meta was awfully sure of her opinions. She put away some rice and chicken. "What do you think of this, Mr. Creech," she asked him. "After I have been in America or when I have been at home, I think how much more complicated existence is there—not an original thought, of course." Creech felt his eyes glaze over at this familiar idea, but he hoped Meta didn't notice. "At home," she said, "most never worry about enough to eat or if it rains where they will sleep, so they must invent worry. Am I good, they worry, or am I bad? Am I unknown to those I love? Does God really care about me? Here life is not troubled in that way because it is reduced to essentials. It is an almost scandalous thing to think, but I am conscious of finding it bracing. I do notice it."

"There's nothing bracing about poverty," Creech replied. "It's simply desperate, here or anywhere else. At best it's just boring, and generations of it produces a psychosis in people that would take a thousand years to unravel. *That's* what you notice."

Creech sounded a bit too stern to himself. He made a point to smile politely, and politely Meta smiled back.

"I am a dithering old bat," Meta said, again with a hard *t* in *bat* that made the word sound like *badd*. She pushed her empty plate away from her and sat back in her chair with her hands folded in her lap. "I don't say what I mean," she said. "I did not mean I find it bracing in the sense that a hike in the mountains is bracing, and afterward you drive home to your dinner. Bracing," she said, "in the sense of glimpsing something *hidden* most of the time." Meta paused to let that thought sink in. Creech waited for her to go on talking. He was thinking that she had baby-pink skin.

"Isn't it true," said Meta, "wouldn't you say, that when we meet people who inhabit another world—like this one—we suspect they have acquaintance, that's the word, acquaintance with a life we don't know? Why else are we so fascinated with this voodoo and zombies and so on? Because we are in awe of what these people know of such things."

"I'm sure most Haitians are more in awe of what it takes to get my dinner."

"You resist my point. I am a celibate . . . "

"Maybe you should slow down."

"Please listen, Mr. Creech," said Meta in a tone that demanded attention. "I have been noodling this thought for some time. I would like to know what you think."

"I like the word *noodling* used that way." He had enough on his mind as it was, and he did not want to be so serious.

"Listen to me," Meta demanded.

Just as she spoke the young man in charge of dinner, another of Mme. St. Charles' sons apparently, appeared to refill her water glass. Meta blushed; Creech thought she had not seemed the type to blush. Before resuming she watched the boy walk ten paces from the table, although surely he could not have heard or understood enough to know what she was on about.

"Consider sex," she insisted. "I have no acquaintance with it, or know why it drives people so, but does that matter? Can I know enough of what is necessary about it from films and books and what people say? Years ago," she said, watching her own finger run along the edge of the glass tabletop, "I began to wonder if having no knowledge of it kept something important hidden from me—who can know? That is what I'm talking about: we respect people if we suspect they know a secret—especially if we suspect that to know it they may have made a deal with the devil. I am fascinated by the sorcerer and by—I suppose the erotic. Do you understand the point I'm making—voodoo, carnality?" Creech replied that he respected both, to which Meta replied with a smile. "That's a cautious answer," she said. She was teasing him.

They had their coffee together and talked about many other things. Meta was clearly a great talker and a great questioner. Once again she brought the discussion around to his family. She presumed the intimacies of an old friend.

After Meta went up to her room Creech tried using the phone to call his wife. All he managed was a recording of a woman's voice speaking in French and Creole saying the international lines were tied up, try later please. He dialed and dialed again for over an hour until his index finger hurt. A Haitian woman in her nightgown, a guest of the hotel, came back every ten minutes to see if he had relinquished the phone. When she saw that he hadn't she put her hands on her hips to show disapproval, her gown transparent with the light behind her.

Meta came back down once to buy stamps from Mme. St. Charles. "No luck?" she asked.

Mme. St. Charles was in the lounge with some other guests— a young French couple and a Japanese family—watching Florida television picked up on the satellite dish that stared up at the sky from beside the empty pool. The guests were absorbed in a program that appeared to be about a tiny Asian woman diving into a pool over and over, a sports show perhaps.

Feeling frustrated, Creech went up to bed, but not to sleep. There was all-night activity in the streets, voices and laughter and a boom box nearby playing frantic, monotonous music. The fan on the bureau played back and forth, but without effect: the heat weighed on him. He was hot and lonesome in the dark. By four he had finished the last drop of water in the Evian he'd opened that afternoon. As dawn was beginning the neighborhood at last became quiet, and then he slept.

Monday morning Creech dressed in a suit. Before going down to breakfast he walked out on the terrace to savor the early coolness and the view of the harbor. There was a clean, cool haze over the ocean, and the sun felt nourishing. Creech was preparing himself for the day; within an hour the heat would be oppressive and by mid-morning Port-au-Prince would be bustling.

He looked for Meta at breakfast, but she had either not come down yet or had already gone out. When he left at eight-thirty, Roger, the young man who hustled him the day before, appeared again. Roger said good morning. "Are you going into the city?" he asked. When Creech said yes Roger shook his head. "Big manifestation today," he said. He bit his thumbnail. "Everyone takes a holiday." Creech did not know what he meant—what holiday? He hoped it did not mean his appointments would be broken; he planned on leaving the next afternoon. "Well," he told Roger. "We'll see."

Ordinarily on any day but Sunday Port-au-Prince was an uproar of *marchandes* and pedestrians and bus drivers competing for space and shouting for attention, but that morning life was in hiding behind steel-shuttered windows. Here and there a few men stood together in the shadows, out of the sun, but they were the exception and were outnumbered by soldiers—solitary helmeted teenagers in green fatigues standing or sitting on the high curbs, rifles across their laps. They watched. They watched Creech drive past with curiosity, perhaps surprise. Creech was scared. Seldom had he known it to be a disadvantage to be conspicuously both white and American.

Naturally he found it ironic that his first appointment of the day was at the U.S. embassy. The Americans occupied a bright white office building on a neat patch of green lawn, down near the docks at the end of Rue Harry Truman. It looked like a piece of Miami parachuted into the squalor of Port-au-Prince. The embassy had an orderly, imperial presence that stood for safety. So did the tall black Marine who let him inside the gate.

The Americans in the embassy were suspected by Haitians of exerting a determining influence over events. This suspicion was true to a large extent, although not as completely true as generally thought. In Port-au-Prince the embassy was a big place, but in Washington, which in those days was obsessively focused on Central America, Port-au-Prince was a forgotten backwater. This situation permitted characters to flourish in the diplomatic mission, such as Alice Jolibois, nee Adkins, the embassy's commercial liaison.

Alice was waiting to greet him on the other side of the metal detector that morning. Creech liked her because she was boisterous and smart-alecky, like a schoolgirl athlete, not at all stiff-necked like most professional diplomats. She was a big woman who carried her weight well and wore her hair in a two-foot braid. Alice had been posted during the Carter administration and had been married six years to Pepe Jolibois, a member of the mulatto aristocracy and an important man in Port-au-Prince. Under Duvalier poor Pepe spent three months in solitary confinement, punishment for writing an essay critical of the government in an American newspaper. When he came out he was something just this side of psychotic, and for Alice the strain was too much. It was very sad. Creech liked them together and had been to their house, a split-level in a sort of condominium development hidden away up in the hills; you would almost never suspect it was there, which might have been intended. Alice lived alone there now with a maid and shelves of books and a splashing fountain and cold beers.

The embassy staff with whom he'd dealt had variously impressed Creech as either deeply ignorant of the country or exceptionally shrewd; looking back it was hard to know which category to assign Alice. "Welcome back, fella," she said as she took his hand. She spoke with a soft accent; she once said she was from South Carolina.

"What's going on out there? Hi."

"Strike. Nobody was supposed to go out—don't you listen to the radio? The trade unions warned people they'd smash up the windows of anyone out on the road this morning. You're a lucky fella."

"I didn't know what was going on," said Creech. "I was scared to death."

Alice escorted him down the quiet carpeted hallway past a rack full of newspapers and various kinds of literature about U.S. government programs, past a framed color photograph of President Reagan and soothing reproductions of Impressionist paintings. "What I like about this job," Alice remarked as they entered her office, "is there's always something out the window to see. Two days ago three hundred people came down the road following a cow. Somebody said they heard it talking in Carrefourt. You should have seen it," she told Creech. "There was this terrific parade with people banging drums, and the cow was marching along as though she actually knew she was leading the procession."

Alice swayed her shoulders and her head to suggest a cow marching.

"Did you ever get my letter?"

"The post office is still on strike," Alice said with the cheerful fatalism Westerners working in the Third World like to affect. "It's a good thing you phoned me," she said. "I would have stayed home otherwise."

"What do you think?" Creech asked her. "This thing today is not exactly a confidence builder. As a matter of fact it's more or less made up my mind for me."

Kevin McDermott

"Well, don't be hasty," said Alice. "More and more I think things will quiet down once elections are over."

Alice was sitting with her feet up on her office couch. She pushed her shoes off with her toes; Creech noticed she wore no stockings. He also noticed she'd lost weight; her features had a definition that didn't use to be there.

"People I speak to don't believe there will be elections," Creech told her. "When I was down last month nobody I talked to on the street thought so. I don't either. You know these guys are crooks, Alice, and crooks are so unpredictable. It makes it hard to plan," he said. "I'm a citizen, protect my interests," and Alice laughed at his little joke. "What kind of leverage do you exert these days?" he asked, gesturing around the office to indicate that he meant the embassy in general.

Alice shrugged. "Unless you're prepared to use force," she said, "you're always limited. If you're not prepared to use force you can only hope to encourage things to go the way you'd like. The army is the government here and you have to deal with them, even if they are crooks. I assume the military is going to run elections," she said matter-of-factly. "*Someone* is going to be elected, and face it, they're all that's keeping the place from falling into an anarchy right now," she added. "Take what you hear on the street with a grain of salt, Creech. People haven't lost the habit of paranoia. They know they're not controlling their fate, so they assume somebody else must be, some hidden power." Alice bared her teeth like a werewolf and curled up her hands like claws.

"Do you blame them?"

"No. They're right. But I'll bet you a dollar elections take place on schedule."

"I don't want to bet." Creech felt irritable. "What should I tell Bajeux?"

"Tell him hi. It's been ages since I saw him."

Creech was with Alice until past eleven. When he left to go see Bajeux the streets in Port-au-Prince had not yet returned to life; it gave him the creeps to see how so many people could simply vanish like that. On the road going out toward the airport an open truck carrying perhaps a dozen soldiers in back passed him going in the direction of the city. The dusty road was otherwise deserted except for a few women walking at the side or leaning in the doorways of their homes, arms folded, watching.

When he got to Bajeux's place Creech saw that the donkey who had been tethered to the fence the day before had since died. His sad carcass now lay by the roadside just next to the pavement; his snout had already been run over and crushed. Creech wondered who took responsibility for removing dead beasts in Haiti as he walked up and down in front of the building, looking for a way in. The gate was padlocked and the shutters had been rolled down in front of the windows.

It made Creech uneasy to feel so alone at midday. He looked for but did not see Bajeux's car, a sporty black Mazda that Bajeux was very proud of. Just then he heard a heavy screeching of metal right above his head; for an instant his heart stopped. "Hey, hello, Creech!" It was Bajeux sticking his head out from under the shutter of his upstairs window. "Come around to the back and I will let you in."

Like a lot of wealthy men in Port-au-Prince, Bajeux had his capital invested in a number of businesses. In addition to owning this space and leasing part of it—including labor—to Creech, he also had a hand in the coffee trade, in a lumber business and even an ad agency. Bajeux imported farming supplies too, which he stored in a cinderblock addition to the building. The inside of his plant always had a heavy smell of potassium nitrate fertilizer; at home Creech could never go to the local garden store without being reminded of Bajeux. His office was a cluttered room knocked together from fake-walnut panelling to one side of the shop floor; he could keep an eye on things from there. It was furnished with secondhand stuff brought down from his house in Petionville. He worked behind a high wooden desk that Creech remembered his schoolteachers having.

"Creech," said Bajeux, holding up a bottle of Dewar's scotch in a sort of greeting, "have a drink with me."

"It's not even noon yet, Henry. No thanks." Bajeux poured himself a shot and watched the scotch with admiration as he swirled it around in the glass. "Strike over?" Creech asked him. He meant to get right to the point.

"For today," said Bajeux, smiling through his trim grey beard and trying to sound amused. He was a little man with olive skin, and when he smiled his teeth looked white as ivory. "I came armed this morning, Creech—honestly I did," smiling brightly as he said so. "Driving my little girl to school I had a pistol on my lap. By god, if anyone tried to make trouble for me they'd regret it." He laughed and took a sip of his drink. "I was prepared to defy heaven to get through my gate this morning, but when I arrived there was no one here—no unionists and no employees, no one to shoot." He collected some shipping documents on his desk, tidied the edges and smiled again. "Here I am, all alone."

"What about tomorrow?" Creech asked him. With a salesman like Bajeux the trick was to keep to the subject. "Will your people be in tomorrow?"

"Yes," said Bajeux, "that's the routine. And then next week, or the week after, something else. My employees are scared," he said passively, shrugging his shoulders. "If they don't come to work they lose a day's pay. If they come to work maybe they are beaten up or worse. A man like me can absorb the loss, but they are afraid. They listen to the one they fear most, and they don't come to work. They are conditioned to live in fear, Creech. The trade unions," he said, warming to his subject and giving Creech his friendly-fellow smile, "see themselves as big democrats, big revolutionaries. They demand I pay higher wages, provide a doctor, paid vacations—Disneyland, Creech. They don't see how they drive jobs away. So irresponsible." He had clearly been rehearsing this all morning. "And now you come to tell me you are pulling out," he said at last, recognizing from Creech's silence that the American wanted to stick to business. "You are going to Mexico. Adios, Haiti—is that correct?"

"It looks like we'd be foolish to stay, doesn't it?" said Creech, wanting to sound both friendly and frank at once. "We're a month behind, and you can't guarantee we'll make it up, can you?"

"No," said Bajeux.

"How secure are those boxes of coupons out there?" Creech asked, pressing his point. "If someone was smart they'd put a match to them. Then we'd really be up a creek. With *you*. Mexico's expensive, but it's stable. You've tried to hold up your end of the bargain, Henry, I know, but it's not working out."

"I realize that." Bajeux surrendered so easily that he must have already resigned himself to this news before Creech arrived.

Bajeux got up and went to the window. It was still partially occluded by the shutter and he had to bend with his hands on his knees to look out. Creech could see part of the dusty shoulder of the road from where he sat; it looked awfully hot out there. "God will not smile on Haiti," said Bajeux, almost without interest like a man talking about the prospect for rain.

"Too much black magic around here," Creech said meanly. "It just annoys Him."

"Yes, we should all have been Protestants," Bajeux answered, still peeking out at the road. "That would have been better." He looked over his shoulder at Creech and smiled without parting his lips.

In Haiti it was easy for Europeans and Americans to travel about within a bubble of other whites, or almost whites like Bajeux, doing business or doing politics or employing power in some other way; the majority of the population remained black and invisible. Sometimes after he came home from Port-au-Prince Creech would think that, except to buy a newspaper or a package of sugarcane on the street, he had spoken to no one who was not just like him, and so he had not really been anywhere at all.

By mid-afternoon the general strike was declared a success and Port-au-Prince came out of hiding. There were few cars or buses out, but a swarm of people filled the streets and transformed them into pedestrian thoroughfares. Poking through the crowded streets in his car Creech was enveloped in the smells of Port-au-Prince, of sweat and unfiltered car exhaust and raw sewage running red/grey in the gutters of the street. Creech felt an almost festive atmosphere. The vendors were out, and boys were kicking a soccer ball in the street in front of the presidential palace. A one-legged kid on crutches was delighting his friends with tricky ball handling, and when Creech tapped his horn the players parted resentfully for his car. A woman slept on the meridian that divided the middle of the road. *Un homme et une femme* was on the marquee of the cinema near the Holiday Inn.

Creech came back to the St. Charles about three. He had half expected to see Roger waiting by the front of the hotel when he pulled in, but he saw no one. There appeared to be no one inside the hotel either, although the television was on in the lounge. The General was on TV, his fat face round under a polished helmet. Alone on camera he seemed to be talking just to Creech as he explained that subversion by leftists, those who had called the strike that morning, had made it necessary for the junta to take a firmer hand. That meant postponing elections and curtailing certain rights of citizens. It made Creech sad. He should have taken Alice's bet.

Where was everyone? From the direction of the kitchen came the voices of people working. He heard the cleaning woman bouncing her cart down the stairs to the lobby.

Creech went up to his room and changed into a swimsuit. Taking a bottle of Evian with him he went out on the veranda to nap in the sun, and having slept poorly the night before his eyes very quickly felt heavy. Soon he fell into a light sleep. He began dreaming of Bajeux, him at the wheel of a big black jeep behind smoked windows. Creech was his passenger. Creech wanted to get out because he had his plane home to catch, but Bajeux insisted with that smile of his that he must show him one more thing, always one more thing, he would find it of interest. Bajeux drove farther and farther into the country, past banana farms, past gaudy voodoo cemeteries. He would never let Creech go home. He was never going to let him out.

Creech awoke in a sticky sweat. The sun by then had moved behind the top of the hotel. He was now in shade, but the inside of one knee had been burned pink. He sat up, drank some water and tried to read the fat American best-seller someone had left behind in his room.

Going down for supper Creech bumped into Meta in the hallway. "Well, hello," she said. "Did you have a successful day?"

"I don't think successful is quite the word for it," Creech answered. "Did you hear about the coup?"

Meta replied that the nuns had watched the General on television that afternoon at the convent where they were holding their meeting. She and Creech talked about it over dinner, about what a mess it all was, and how sad. Creech told her what he knew of Haiti's history of tenuous government, and somehow ended by telling her about his dream of riding with Bajeux and of his visit with him that morning.

"What happens to the workers then, the ones sorting your coupons?" Meta asked.

"Probably not much," said Creech. Thinking about it depressed him. "For some of them Bajeux might find work doing something else," he told her. "We'll pay some sort of separation benefit to keep our fences mended in case we ever decide to come back, but who knows how much of that Bajeux's employees will ever see. You've probably gathered that I don't trust Bajeux. I never liked having to work with him." He chuckled and gave Meta a wry smile, just the way Bajeux might do. "Tonight I guess it's my turn to hold the floor."

"How do you mean—'hold the floor'?"

"You know," said Creech, "talk a lot, like a person at a public gathering. It's a common expression," he assured her.

"I will have to add it to my colloquialisms."

Creech laughed, glad to have Meta's company. He asked her how her day had been. "Well," she said, "much of our talk is very general. I suspect the true reason we come together," she said smiling, "is that our work is lonely. We are typically the only Westerners in the places where we live, and almost always the only women of—what?—education?"

Meta paused to take a forkful of rice and chopped meat. "Do you remember," she asked Creech, speaking with her mouth full, "do you remember what we spoke about last evening, when I held the floor and talked about knowledge of the world?"

"Your curiosity about secret things?"

"More than curiosity, Mr. Creech," Meta corrected him. "My *respect* for secret things. You said that yourself."

"Yes, I remember what we said."

"At the convent where we are meeting," she told him, "there is a school for girls. They are learning useful skills from the sisters, and are being prepared for a religious life. At the lunch hour this afternoon the girls performed a chorale for us. They were so pretty and young," Meta said. "Do you notice, Mr. Creech, that Haitians are a very handsome people?"

"Yes, I think that too," Creech agreed; he enjoyed the way Meta interrupted herself to comment on something she had just said.

"I felt sad at the sight of these girls," Meta confided. "One often has such a response to beauty, I understand, yet it caused me to recall what I said to you about having knowledge. I had a sudden insight that the life for which they are being trained is in some way divorcing them—I believe that's the correct expression—from what is strongest in them."

"The girls are blessed in getting an education," Creech said. "That should make you glad."

"It does make me glad, certainly glad," said Meta. "I do not mean to say they would be better off ignorant."

"I hope not."

"I was remembering how I was at their age." Meta was almost too much in earnest. "I believe it is wrong," she said, "that these girls will never have the experience of a romantic love, Mr. Creech. Wrong for their souls."

"You regret never having married, don't you? Is that it, you regret that?"

Kevin McDermott

"Marriage," Meta replied, "who knows? Perhaps it would not appeal to me. I am talking about a knowledge of sex."

"Oh."

"It would fill out their characters," she said. "Among the saints, I always have a special attraction to Thomas Merton. His character was full, and I think it was because of his sex experiences as a young man."

"I don't have much knowledge of saints," said Creech. People who talked about religion always seemed to take conversation down to dead ends.

"I use the term in the meaning of someone having hidden knowledge," Meta explained, "of knowing the one great thing. Merton was greatly torn between life in the world and his wish for a life of meditation. Prayer," she began to say, but they were interrupted just then by the noise of drums. The drumming was accompanied by a low, deep groaning. It was the sound of people humming, and it was coming from the direction of the street. They got up from the table and went to the edge of the porch to look out, peering into the absolute dark. Two French couples who had also been having dinner joined them. They could see nothing, nothing out in the night but the movement of flickering candlelight as the procession moved closer and the humming grew louder. Unseen, the drummers beat a quiet, complex rhythm as the ceremony moved past the St. Charles, out in the darkness. As he stood with Meta and the others, Creech felt suddenly too far from his family and awfully alone, as far as he had felt that morning driving through empty streets in town, alone as he had felt trying to find a way into Bajeux's place.

"What is it?" Meta asked. The French also turned toward Creech expectantly, as though he knew something. But Creech said, "I don't know."

The procession headed slowly down the hill and out of the neighborhood. When it had moved on everyone went back to their table and finished their coffee, but the atmosphere had been left unsettled. Meta did not resume her talk about sex and the rest of it, nor did Creech push her back in that direction. He felt the common aversion to being cornered by someone else's loneliness, and Meta seemed to be a woman with a big idea of missed happiness nagging at her.

After coffee they said goodnight. Before she went upstairs Meta asked Creech if he would be kind enough to drop her at the convent on his way to the airport the next morning; the other sister with whom she had ridden that day had abruptly left the country for a family emergency. Creech said he'd be glad to give her a lift.

Later he tried telephoning his wife again, but this time he gave up after only half an hour.

About ten o'clock Meta rapped on the door of his room. She stood in the hallway wearing her night dress and a bathrobe. "I'm glad to see you're awake," she said. "I hope I'm not bothering you."

"I was just reading. Anything the matter?"

"No, not at all," Meta said. "Do you have a moment? There is something I would like to show you."

Creech followed Meta back down the hall to her room. She closed the door behind them, giving him a sly smile and a friendly glance out the corner of her eye. The room was suffused with a woman scent of lotions and soap. Meta went to her suitcase at the window and took out a small travel case, a gaudy yellow thing meant for toiletries and makeup. She unzipped the case and took out some thing wrapped in clear plastic. It was a photograph. She removed it from the plastic by its edges and handed it to Creech. It was an old polaroid on which the color had faded badly, but it was still quite a vivid scene. It showed two dark-skinned men—policemen perhaps, to judge by their uniforms. They were looking up at the camera in surprise as they crouched over the naked body of a white man. The man was clearly dead. His penis was erect but his mouth was slack and his eyes did not reflect the camera's flash like the dark eyes of the policemen.

"What is this?" Creech asked as he studied the picture, feeling his flesh shiver a little.

Meta was smiling at him. "That is Thomas Merton in death," she told him. "It was given to me by a dear friend, a Swiss nun who has died. She knew of my interest in Merton and generously gave this to me. She photographed it herself just after they found him." She turned her eyes to the photograph. A look of melancholy came across her face. "Apparently he electrocuted himself while showering," she said. "He was at a gathering rather like the one that I am attending here in Port-au-Prince, in a place that would remind one of Haiti. It's a relic."

"Why do you keep a thing like this?" said Creech. "It's so upsetting."

"I employ it," Meta replied, "to meditate on his humanity. I find the way of his death—an accident, in the shower of all places—so touching. I am convinced he would have found it comical."

Meta looked at him and smiled, but Creech could not find a reply. He merely nodded to show that he was listening and handed Meta's picture back to her. She took one edge between her fingers and with loving care replaced the photograph in the plastic wrap. Her expression seemed almost beatific, a look of kindness, of great love.

"Well, I can honestly say I've never seen anything like that," said Creech, trying to manage a small joke. He was trying to break his own tension. He was absolutely at a loss for words. He was extremely uncomfortable and fought a welling sense of real fright. "I'll see you at breakfast then," he said, and he retreated down the hall to his bed.

Creech and Meta left early in the morning while the day was still cool. Roger, whom Creech had looked for the afternoon before, was sitting at the curbside when they left, poking at the street with a stick. Creech tooted his horn and Roger looked up. He waved.

Coming down the hill they were detoured by a crew of telephone repairmen. The men had pulled the wires down from the poles, and the wires lay in a snakey chaos all over the road. A limb had been rudely broken off a nearby tree and lain across the street as a barrier. Meta instructed Creech to turn right and head up Rue John Paul II. They fell in behind a green jeep carrying armed soldiers. The jeep crawled along at less than twenty miles an hour to allow the soldiers to survey the deliberately blank faces of the people at the side of the road stealing glances at them as they passed by. Creech decided he wouldn't try to pass.

He and Meta followed the street to a place where the pavement stopped, where Meta directed him to continue up the hill on a dirt road. The road was rutted and gullied and gave the underside of the car a terrible hammering; later, when Creech was driving to the airport, the car would rattle and screech as if it were coming apart. On one side the road fell off in a sheer drop straight down to houses clustered at the bottom of the hillside.

The convent was a simple collection of stucco buildings at the top of the hill. It was surrounded by a wall seven feet high; colorful shards of broken bottles were set in cement along the top to keep anyone from grabbing hold. Men were not permitted inside through the wall, Meta explained to Creech; she asked if he would please wait. She said she had a present to give his wife.

The sun was well up by then. It was hot as Creech waited, and his car's chrome and the stoney ground gave back a harsh glare. Creech got out and stretched his legs. He looked down from the hill at the city and the harbor; from up high Port-au-Prince unaccountably reminded him of Naples. He looked at his watch. It was nearly ten and his plane left at noon. Meta had already been gone for more than fifteen minutes and he was getting anxious. While he was waiting a small boy appeared from somewhere. He had a full head of rust-colored hair, which Creech knew was a symptom of malnutrition. He smiled. "*Salut,*" said Creech, smiling back. Encouraged, the little boy spoke to him, but in Creole and so rapidly that Creech had no idea of what he was saying. "*J'attendant pour mon ami,*" he tried. "*Elle est une soeur,*" patting the roof with his hand. The boy said something else. He seemed to be indicating the car. "*Il est ma voiture,*" Creech acknowledged. He searched his brain for a moment for a way of expressing "rental" in French, and then wondered if the boy would understand the concept.

Creech was concerned that he would miss his flight if he waited much longer. He knew he ought just to leave, yet had a powerful sense that he would be somehow stranding Meta if he went without saying goodbye; it was necessary. The other side of the wall might be forbidden, but the nuns would simply have to cope with the shock of a man in their midst. Surely they would not shoot him.

Creech said *au revoir* to the little boy and hopped up on the car's hood to see over the gate into the church yard. He saw a red rooster and a tidy garden and washing drying on a line, but no people. He could not wait any longer. Stepping up from the car to the top of the gate, he hopped over and landed in the yard; half to his surprise, he was not immediately struck by lightning. He walked toward the building that looked most like a school and entered a cloistered walk. As he did he glimpsed Meta just passing into a doorway at the other end. He walked down and found the same door. When he opened it he saw Meta there, standing at the head of a long table surrounded by young girls, all in identical pale blue jumpers. An old nun in a copious habit sat in a chair against the wall behind Meta. They were praying, and with one surprised glance they took him in and then turned away.

He immediately retreated, embarrassed but also miffed at having been forgotten. He was already halfway back to the gate when Meta came calling after him, "Mr. Creech! Mr. Creech!" When she caught up to him she apologized. "The girls insisted I say the rosary with them," she explained, a little out of breath. "It was very flattering, but I did not expect to be delayed. I know you have an airplane to catch."

Creech said that was all right, but he had to hurry now. He wished Meta a good trip back to the Philippines. "But wait," she said. "I promised you something for your wife." She searched in her skirt pocket and found a tiny envelope. "Open it," she said. Creech did as he was told and took out a small religious medal with a woman's head engraved on it. The head was covered with a sort of wimple. "That is a representation of Erzulie Freda, the vudon goddess of love," Meta told him. "A Belgian priest explained it to me. Really it's the Virgin Mother," she said, "but it's a case where the two traditions overlap. Please give it to your wife. Tell her it's a love charm," she added slyly. "Perhaps she can use it to keep you at home."

That was in 1987, and the charm has worked ever since. Creech has never been back to Haiti; confusion was just too much a part of life there.

Even while checking in for his flight that morning he sensed that he would not be returning; everywhere he turned, it seemed, he caught the eye of someone staring at him. At the windows of the waiting area the faces of those with relatives departing for New York pressed against the glass, searching for the ones they knew. Creech could not watch them without feeling that they watched him back. It made him uneasy.

He had the same sensation as the plane taxied to the top of the runway. Peering out through the little porthole at the crush of people standing at the chain-link fence he thought of how they must have envied him his freedom to fly away. The people stood motionless at the barrier, watching as the plane flew off for the magic place.

Kevin McDermott is the managing editor of *D&B Reports* and has written for *The Washington Post*, *The Atlantic Monthly*, *Business Week*, and elsewhere. This is his first short story to appear in the United States.

GEEZERS / *Ursula K. Le Guin*

T HE IDEA OF DRIVING OVER to the coast for the weekend came to him as a revelation—what his English professor used to call an epiphany. Actually it came to him from Debi, his personal secretary. "You look *so* tired, Warren," she said. "Last weekend, I left the kids with Pat and went over to Lincoln City and found a motel, and I just sat there with a dumb novel for a whole afternoon, and went to bed at nine, and in the morning I had this long walk on the beach. I must of gone a mile. It made all the difference. In case you noticed how cheerful and brilliant I've been all week." Although he did not always get the details, he generally listened to Debi; and this time what she had said, even the words, came to him, as an epiphany, while he was driving home.

Saturday was lunch with the Curry County commissioner about South County development, but a phone call put that off till Tuesday. He got back into the car in jeans and windbreaker, with pyjamas, running shoes, sweats, and a toothbrush in his briefcase, and took off.

He knew he was a creature of habit, stuck in every rut he got into. He knew that was why he was effective, got things done. But Debi was right, he needed a break. And the fact was that because he was so steady and routine, when he broke loose and did some thing out of the ordinary he *appreciated* it, savored it to the full. Since the divorce he hadn't given himself much to savor. But now he was free, and he wasn't even going to go to Lincoln City, but farther, to find some hidden place, a discovery. "I found this incredible little place over on the coast...." The Cutlass flew through the winding Wilson River gorges—God, it was beautiful, he ought to get out of town more often—to Tillamook Junction. A toss-up, 101 south to Tijuana or north to Fairbanks. He did not hesitate. Fancy free, he sped north.

He had forgotten that 101 ran inland for a good way north of Tillamook. By the time he got back out to the coast the sun had set and motel signs in the little towns said NO and SORRY. When he saw the sign for Klatsand, Pop 351, Please Drive Carefully, he took the chance and turned off the highway. There'd be something down in town.

There was: the White Gull, VACANCY, marigolds in wooden boxes brightening the twilight.

"You're lucky," said the short woman at the desk, with a smile that grudged him his luck. "They booked the whole place. But they're two short, and they only pay for what they get. It's two nights minimum. Fourteen's the end one, across there." She pushed the key at him with no questions about what he wanted and no information concerning the cost. He was lucky. He accepted the luck and the key and put down his credit card. A lot of people in Salem would have recognized his name, but not over here in the boonies. The woman (John and Mary Brinnesi, Your Hosts, Are Pleased to Welcome You) ran the imprinter over the card with a heavy hand. "Have a nice day," she said, although it was nearly nine at night. "Park anywhere. They're all in the bus."

What she meant, evidently, was that the other people staying at the White Gull had all come on the huge bus that loomed across four or five parking spaces. Walking along beside it on his way to Number Fourteen, he read the sign that ran along under its windows:

The Sightseeing Seniors of Cedarwood
A Christian Community

It'll be a quiet night at the White Gull, he thought with amusement. He looked over the clean room, its king-size bed, its gypsy dancer on black velvet and schooner in the sunset, smelled its bubble-gum disinfectant, and went out to dinner. Coming into town he had noticed a place called Mayfield's, a promising name; he had a flair for little places. Mayfield's was bigger than it looked from outside, and rather elegant, with white tablecloths and hurricane-lamp candles. It was also quite full, voices crowding warmly under the beamed ceiling. A boy hurried to seat him—
"Are you with the group, sir?"

"No, no," Warren said, smiling.

"I thought you were kind of late if you were," the boy said, ingenuous, leading him to a small dark table under a Boston fern. "They're mostly on dessert. I'm Jason. Would you like something from the bar?"

Rose Ellen, who looked like she might be Jason's mother, brought Warren a glass of Chardonnay. While he waited for his grilled Chinook he watched the Sightseeing Seniors. They sat by fours and sixes; they were merry, convivial, grey and white and bald heads bobbing in the candlelight. They shouted stories from table to table and laughed aloud. There wasn't a wine glass on any table but his own. Strong in their numbers, they acted like they owned the place, but they were having such a good time, who could blame them? And suddenly his sleeve was plucked; a nice-looking old lady at the next table was leaning over and smiling. "If you'd like to join us, you know, you just do that. We're terribly noisy!"

"Oh, no, thanks so much," Warren said, with his fundraising smile. "I'm just enjoying listening to you all."

"Well, you looked so lonesome sitting there, and I just didn't like to think you might feel left out," the old lady said, and nodded reassuringly, and turned away.

These are the salt of the earth, Warren said to himself, as his salmon arrived. These are Americans.

A few of them left while he was eating. They stopped by one table or another to say goodnight and make more jokes. There seemed to be an infallible subject of hilarity, something to do with Wayne and trout fishing, and when Wayne himself left, shouting, "See you at the fishing hole!" gales of laughter swept the room. Most of them were still there, some still eating cake and drinking coffee, when Warren slipped out with a nod to the nice lady at the next table. She smiled and said, "You take care, now."

His room had no sea view, but he could hear the breakers just over the dunes. He had stuffed a folder on the Amonson committee in his briefcase under the running shoes, but after looking at it for five minutes he turned on the big TV set and watched the last half of a detective show. Finding he had slept right through the gunfire, he brushed his teeth and went to bed. Faint sounds of Seniors parting before their doors blended with the long in-out, in-out of the sea. He slept.

He woke, where? Banging on the door—what door?—"Oh, excuse me! Gee, I thought Jerry and Alice were in this one. Ex-cuse us!" Retreating laughter.

It was a little before seven. He lay a while luxuriating, then got up ready for a run on the beach. He thought of Debi, so proud of walking a mile. Most women past a certain age didn't keep themselves fit. He felt tremendously fit this morning.

Ater the dim motel room with its lined curtains the sweep of the morning sky dazzled him. Shadows of the dunes lay cool and blue across the sand, but the foaming breakers and the sea burned like salt fire in the summer light. All up and down the beach, though it wasn't seven-thirty yet, people walked and jogged in pairs and groups. As he trotted by they nodded and greeted him,

Ursula K. Le Guin

"Morning!" "Morning!" They were bald or grey, in purple sweats and flowered shirts. They were Seniors, keeping fit.

A young man and woman flashed by at a run, running like deer. He jogged after them. Their double footprints in the sand were at twice the interval of his own. As he kept on, the Seniors began to thin out. By the time he was halfway to the big rock that closed off the beach at the south he had it all to himself, except for the young couple, who sped back past him without a glance, talking continuously in clear, unwinded voices.

It was a long way to the rock. He got his breath there, sitting on a black boulder over tidepools, and then jogged back slowly. No need to push it. The beach was now empty as if new-created, made for him alone, the first man. He was grateful.

He showered and went to find breakfast.

Tom's Seaside Grill looked like the place for breakfast, red checked tablecloths, bustling waitresses.

"Your party's in the garden room, sir," said the fair, plump girl with the menus.

"I'm not with them," Warren said with a flash of irritation.

"I see, this way then," said the girl, woundingly uninterested, and took him to a front window table. From it he watched all Klatsand pass.

As the occupants of the garden room left in pairs and groups and stood about in front of Tom's, it appeared that all Klatsand consisted of Sightseeing Seniors; but of course, Warren thought, these small beach communities had a large percentage of retired population year-round. Thinking about taxation demography, he was relieved to see a young woman with two toddlers go by. And there was a couple, not exactly young but anyway not old. And dogs—large, free, joyous dogs, beach dogs—went by, stopping now and then politely to greet a Senior.

The menu had a Senior Special across the top, one piece bacon or sausage, no-cholesterol Egg-O, wheat toast, lo-cal spread, and prunes.

Warren ordered two over easy with home fries. The coffee was warm brown bitter water, but the food was hot and succulent, hi-cal.

I'll work this morning and sit on the beach this afternoon, he told himself. He liked to know what he was going to do, to dig his rut, even for a day. He strolled back to the White Gull, happy. The marigolds blazed. "Hey there! Terrific day!" somebody greeted him. He tried to place him—County? State?—this imposing old man with a broad, bald, brown head, then realized it was Wayne, the trout fisherman.

"Well, hi!" he said. He almost added, "Going fishing?" but did not. It would have pleased the old geezer, but he wanted, he did not know quite why, he wanted not to be *involved* with them.

He read, made notes, drafted a proposal. Though the light in the room was annoyingly dim, the work went fast and easily here, with no distractions, and all at once it was one o'clock. He had worked off that big breakfast and was hungry. He went back up to Main Street and walked up one side and down the other of its three commercial blocks, appreciating the sunlit, salt-bitten, grey-shingled shops and houses, all one-storeyed; no neon; no fast-food chains. They had a smart town council here, with a policy. Edna's Dory diner looked like a good bet for lunch. He checked through the window first. Edna's was nearly empty: a couple with a baby at one table. No grey, white, or bald heads. There were only six tables. He went in. A woman shaped like a section of log covered with a short dress and apron greeted him from the kitchen doorway: "Your group's over at the Dancing Sand-Dab," she said sternly.

"I don't have a group," he answered equally sternly.

"Oh, sorry," she said, not sounding sorry. "I just thought. Well, sit anywhere." She vanished into the kitchen. He sat.

The sole was heavily breaded and had been fried in grease for a long time. He knew in his heart that the Dancing Sand-Dab had light, delicate, lo-cal sole.

After lunch he walked around town, happy again, conscious of being happy. He looked at souvenirs in windows. He would come back and get one of those sandcastle ashtrays for Debi. She still smoked, though not on the job, of course. He played with the idea of buying one of the little houses east of Main, serene in their weedy gardens and grey paling fences, sunlight on their silvery shake roofs. It wasn't old money, of course, like Gearhart, or a prestige location, like Salishan, but it had a kind of quiet class. A house in Klatsand would be an interesting statement. Independent. That's my trademark, he thought, independence. I don't go with the group.

Wandering astray, he found he had to cross a strange, marshy area and skirt a black wood of heavily drooping trees to get back to the dunes. The dunes were higher here south of the main part of town. He climbed; his shoes filled instantly with sand. He came out above the broad sweep of beach, already familiar: the

Ursula K. Le Guin

big rock at the south end, the high green headland at the north, the Seniors dotted all about in shorts and swimsuits, wading, sunbathing, playing volleyball.

He found himself a hollow in the dunes from which he could just see the ocean, but not the beach. Shouts and laughter from afar mingled with the soft thunder of the breakers. It was incredibly hot in the hollow, though the seawind blew over it making the feathery heads of the dune grass nod. After twenty minutes he knew he had to get either some sunblock or a hat.

He had noticed a little pharmacy on Spruce Street. He climbed back over the dunes and walked along the wide, sandy road between them and the front row of houses. A beachfront property was the most desirable, but even in a place like this the price would be pretty stiff. A good investment, though, now that Californians were buying up the south coast. Actually he liked some of those little houses on the other side of Main better, but they were pretty much retirement-income-type places. It was too bad.

The girl behind the counter in the small drugs and souvenirs and postcards and taffy shop was beautiful: a dark-eyed redhead, luminous. She did not speak, but he was aware of her presence as he looked over the terrible terrycloth hats by the door and then idled along the shelves, reading the protection factors on tubes of sunblock, glancing at her now and then. When at last he brought his selection to the counter she smiled at him, and he smiled back. She wore a black plastic tag with her name in gold: Irma.

"You people are really having a time of it!" Irma said. "I think it's just wonderful."

Warren's heart seemed to drop or sink physically, an inch or more, inside his chest.

"I work in Salem," he said.

It sounded strange.

"This is a nice town," he said.

She knew something was amiss, but didn't know what. "It's real quiet," she said. "And four makes ten. Have a good day now! Take care!"

I'm only fifty-two! Warren cried out to her in despairing silence.

The sunblock in its little paper bag was in his hand, but he could not go back to the beach with the frolicking Seniors. He struck out north up Lewis Street, then along Fir Street to Clark Street. There was a little park back in here, he had noticed after lunch. He would sit in the park and put sunblock on his forehead and nose.

He did so, sitting on a bench in the dappled shade of the big, black, droopy trees that grew around here. He was unaccountably tired, even sleepy. But that was what he'd come here for, to relax, after all. Gulls yiped, crows croaked, children's voices called across the sunlit, weedy grass of Klatsand City Park. An intermittent droning, bumping noise must be the sound of the ocean coming and going on the wind. Above a vast bank of rhododendrons with purple flowers a small child appeared, flying. Presently it appeared again, flying, in the same direction. It was such a pleasant sight, a flying child, that Warren in his hebetude of weariness and sunlight simply accepted it.

A second and larger child in a red, white, and blue striped rugby shirt flew over the rhododendrons in the same direction, with the same rise and dip, like a swallow.

Warren sighed a little, getting up. He did not hurry. A third child soared past as he crossed the grass and walked around the thicket of rhododendrons.

The City of Klatsand had built for its children a skateboard rink—an oval of cement with a steeply slanted wall shaped like the figure 3—and the children of Klatsand flew about that wall and up into the air, with a light drone and clap of wheels, one after another, like swallows from a cliff.

Warren watched them with the earnest, stupid absorption of a sleepy man. They were beautiful and almost entirely silent. They flew, came down, came round on the grass with skateboard under arm, and waited in line to fly again.

Near Warren one boy stood, skateboard under arm but not in line.

"Looks like fun," Warren said, unsmiling, softly.

"Kids," the boy said.

He was, Warren realized, a couple of years older than the flying children. Maybe more, maybe four or five years older. Maybe a teenager.

"They don't like it when we take over," the boy said, tolerantly. He had never looked at Warren. He did not have to. He said nothing more. In the shade of the rhododendrons sat several other boys his age, waiting to take over.

Warren stood and watched the children flying until the heat of the sun beat in his temples. He went back then to the motel. Mrs. Brinnesi was out front, pulling up tiny weeds from the boxes of marigolds. "Too hot down on the beach for you?" she said with her vindictive smile, and he said, "Guess it is," though she must have seen that he wasn't even coming from the beach.

The nice lady, the one who had invited him to join her table, was letting herself in at Number Sixteen. She smiled at him. "Well, hi there! Have you been enjoying yourself?"

"Yes," said Warren, surrendering. "Have you?"

"Oh, yes! But the beach is so hot today."

"I went to the park. Watched the kids skateboarding."

"Oh! yes, they are so bad, those skateboards!" she said with hearty assurance of their being in agreement—"come up behind you before you know it and could just knock you off your feet! They ought to be banned. Illegal."

"Yes," said Warren, "well." He unlocked his door. "Have a good day," he said.

"Oh, I will!" she said. "Take care, now!"

Ursula K. Le Guin has published fifteen novels and about sixty short stories. This story is part of a collection, *Searoad*, to be out soon by HarperCollins.

ADVANCED BIOLOGY / *Judith Ortiz Cofer*

A S I LAY OUT MY clothes for the trip to Miami to do a reading from my recently published novel, then on to Puerto Rico to see my mother, I take a close look at my wardrobe—the tailored skirts in basic colors easily coordinated with my silk blouses—I have to smile to myself remembering what my mother had said about my conservative outfits when I visited her the last time—that I looked like the Jehovah's Witnesses who went from door to door in her pueblo trying to sell tickets to heaven to the die-hard Catholics. I would scare people she said. They would bolt their doors if they saw me approaching with my briefcase. As for her, she dresses in tropical colors—a red skirt and parakeet-yellow blouse look good on her tan skin, and she still has a good enough figure than she can wear a tight, black cocktail dress to go dancing at her favorite club, El Palacio, on Saturday nights. And, she emphasizes, still make it to the 10 o'clock mass on Sunday. Catholics can have fun and still be saved, she has often pointed out to me, but only if you pay your respects to God and all His Court with the necessary rituals. She has never accepted my gradual slipping out of the faith in which I was so strictly brought up.

As I pack my clothes into the suitcase, I recall our early days in Paterson, New Jersey, where we lived for most of my adolescence while my father was alive and stationed in Brooklyn Yard in New York. At that time, my mother's views on everything from clothing to (the forbidden subject) sex were ruled by the religious fervor that she had developed as a shield against the cold foreign city. These days we have traded places in a couple of areas since she has "gone home" after my father's death, and "gone native." I chose to attend college in the U.S. and make a living as an English teacher and, lately, on the lecture circuit as a free-lance writer. But, though our lives are on the surface radically different, my mother and I have affected each other reciprocally over the past twenty years; she has managed to liberate herself from the rituals, mores and traditions that "cramp" her style, while retaining her femininity and "Puertoricanness," while I struggle daily to consolidate my opposing cultural identities. In my adolescence, divided into my New Jersey years and my Georgia years, I received an education in the art of cultural compromise.

In Paterson in the 1960s I attended a public school in our neighborhood. Still predominantly white and Jewish, it was rated very well academically in a city where the educational system was in chaos, deteriorating rapidly as the best teachers moved on to suburban schools following the black and Puerto Rican migration into, and the white exodus from, the city proper.

The Jewish community had too much at stake to make a fast retreat; many of the small businesses and apartment buildings in the city's core were owned by Jewish families of the World War II generation. They had seen worse things happen than the influx of black and brown people that was scaring away the Italians and the Irish. But they too would gradually move their families out of the best apartments in their buildings and into houses in East Paterson, Fairlawn, and other places with lawns. It was how I saw the world then; either you lived without your square of grass, or you bought a house to go with it. But for most of my adolescence, I lived among the Jewish people of Paterson. We rented an apartment owned by the Milsteins, proprietors also of the deli on the bottom floor. I went to school with their children. My father took his business to the Jewish establishments, perhaps because these men symbolized "dignified survival" to him. He was obsessed with privacy, and could not stand the personal turns conversations almost always took when two or more Puerto Ricans met casually over a store counter. The Jewish men talked too, but they concentrated on externals. They asked my father about his job, politics, his opinion on Vietnam, Lyndon Johnson. And my father, in his quiet voice, answered their questions knowledgeably. Sometimes before we entered a store, the cleaners, or a shoe-repair shop, he would tell me to look for the blue-inked numbers on the owner's left forearm. I would stare at these numbers, now usually faded enough to look like veins in the wrong place. I would try to make them out. They were a telegram from the past, I later decided, informing the future of the deaths of millions. My father discussed the Holocaust with me in the same hushed tones my mother used to talk about God's Mysterious Ways. I could not reconcile both in my mind. This conflict eventually led to my first serious clash with my mother over irreconcilable (I have since learned not to broach certain subjects with her and my other staunchly Catholic relatives) differences between the "real world" and religious doctrine.

It had to do with the Virgin Birth.

And it had to do with my best friend and study partner, Ira

Nathan, the acknowledged scientific genius at school. In junior high school it was almost a requirement to be "in love" with an older boy. I was an eighth grader and Ira was in the ninth grade that year and preparing to be sent away to some prep school in New England. I chose him as my boyfriend (in the eyes of my classmates, if a girl spent time with a boy that meant they were "going together") because I needed tutoring in biology—one of his best subjects. I ended up having a crush on him after our first Saturday morning meeting at the library. Ira was my first exposure to the wonders of an analytical mind.

The problem was the subject. Biology is a dangerous topic for young teenagers who are themselves walking laboratories, experimenting with interesting combinations of chemicals every time they make a choice. In my basic biology class, we were looking at single-cell organisms under the microscope, and watching them reproduce in slow-motion films in a darkened classroom. Though the process was as unexciting as watching a little kid blow bubbles, we were aroused by the concept itself. Ira's advanced class was dissecting fetal pigs. He brought me a photograph of his project, inner organs labeled neatly on the paper, the picture had been glued to. My eyes refused to budge from the line drawn from "genitals" to the corresponding part of the pig. I felt a wave of heat rising from my chest to my scalp. Ira must have seen my discomfort, though I tried to keep my face behind the black curtain of my hair, but as the boy-scientist, he was relentless. He actually traced the line from label to pig with his pencil.

"All mammals reproduce sexually," he said in a teacherly monotone.

The librarian, far off on the other side of the room, looked up at us and frowned. Logically, it was not possible that she could have heard Ira's pronouncement, but I was convinced that the mention of sex enhanced the hearing capabilities of parents, teachers and librarians by one hundred percent. I blushed more intensely, and peeked through my hair at Ira.

He was holding the eraser of his pencil on the pig's blurry sexual parts and smiling at me. His features were distinctly Eastern European. I had recently seen the young singer Barbra Streisand on the Red Skelton show and had been amazed at how much similarity there was in their appearances. She could have been his sister. I was particularly attracted to the wide mouth and strong nose. No one that I knew in school thought that Ira was attractive, but his brains had long ago overshadowed his looks as his most impressive attribute. Like Ira, I was also a straight A student and also considered odd because I was one of the few Puerto Ricans on the honor roll. So it didn't surprise anyone that Ira and I had drifted toward each other. Though I could not have articulated it then, Ira was seducing me with his No. 2 pencil and the laboratory photograph of his fetal pig. The following Saturday, Ira brought in his advanced biology book and showed me the transparencies of the human anatomy in full color that I was not meant to see for a couple of more years. I was shocked. The cosmic jump between paramecium and the human body was almost too much for me to take in. These were the first grown people I had ever seen naked and they revealed too much.

"Human sexual reproduction can only take place when the male's sperm is introduced into the female womb and fertilization of the egg takes place," Ira stated flatly.

The book was open to the page labeled "The Human Reproductive System." Feeling that my maturity was being tested, as well as my intelligence, I found my voice long enough to contradict Ira.

"There has been one exception to this Ira." I was feeling a little smug about knowing something that Ira obviously did not.

"Judith, there are no exceptions in biology, only mutations, and adaptations through evolution." He was smiling in a superior way.

"The Virgin Mary had a baby without...." I couldn't say having sex in the same breath as the name of the Mother of God. I was totally unprepared for the explosion of laughter that followed my timid statement. Ira had crumpled in his chair and was laughing so hard that his thin shoulders shook. I could hear the librarian approaching. Feeling humiliated, I started to put my books together. Ira grabbed my arm.

"Wait, don't go," he was still giggling uncontrollably. "I'm sorry. Let's talk a little more. Wait, give me a chance to explain."

Reluctantly, I sat down again mainly because the librarian was already at our table, hands on hips, whispering angrily: "If you children cannot behave in this study area, I will have to ask you to leave." Ira and I both apologized, though she gave him a nasty look because his mouth was still stretched from ear to ear in a hysterical grin.

"Listen, listen. I'm sorry that I laughed like that. I know you're Catholic and you believe in the Virgin Birth (he bit his lower lip trying to regain his composure), but it's just not biologically possible to have a baby without... (he struggled for composure)... losing your virginity."

I sank down on my hard chair. "Virginity." He had said another of the forbidden words. I glanced back at the librarian who was keeping her eye on us. I was both offended and excited by Ira's blasphemy. How could he deny a doctrine that people had believed in for two thousand years? It was part of my prayers every night. My mother talked about La Virgen as if she were one of our most important relatives.

Recovering from his fit of laughter, Ira kept his hand discretely on my elbow as he explained in the seductive language of the scientific laboratory how babies were made, and how it was impossible to violate certain natural laws.

"Unless God will it." I argued feebly.

"There is no God," said Ira, and the last shred of my innocence fell away as I listened to his arguments backed up by irrefutable scientific evidence.

Our meetings continued all that year, becoming more exciting with every chapter in his biology book. My grades improved dramatically since one-celled organisms were no mystery to a student of advanced biology. Ira's warm, moist hand often brushed against mine under the table at the library, and walking home one bitter cold day, he asked me if I would wear his Beta Club pin. I nodded and when we stepped inside the hallway of my building, he removed his thick mittens which his mother had knitted and pinned the blue enamel B to my collar. And to the hissing of the steam heaters, I received a serious kiss from Ira. We separated abruptly when we heard Mrs. Milstein's door open.

"Hello, Ira."

"Hello, Mrs. Milstein."

"And how is your mother? I haven't seen Fritzie all week. She's not sick, is she?"

"She's had a mild cold, Mrs. Milstein. But she is steadily improving." Ira's diction became extremely precise and formal when he was in the presence of adults. As an only child and a prodigy, he had to live up to very high standards.

"I'll call her today," Mrs. Milstein said, finally looking over at me. Her eyes fixed on the collar of my blouse which was, I later saw in our hall mirror, sticking straight up with Ira's pin attached crookedly to the edge.

"Good-bye, Mrs. Milstein."

"Nice to see you, Ira."

Ira waved awkwardly to me as he left. Mrs. Milstein stood in the humid hallway of her building watching me run up the stairs.

Our "romance" lasted only a week; long enough for Mrs. Milstein to call Ira's mother, and for Mrs. Nathan to call my mother. I was subjected to a lecture on moral behavior by my mother, who, carried away by her anger and embarrassed that I had been seen kissing a boy (understood: a boy who was not even Catholic), had begun a chain of metaphors for the loss of virtue that was on the verge of the tragi/comical:

"A perdida, a cheap item," she said trembling before me as I sat on the edge of my bed, facing her accusations, "a girl begins to look like one when she allows herself to be handled by men."

"Mother..." I wanted her to lower her voice so that my father, sitting at the kitchen table reading, would not hear. I had already promised her that I would confess my sin that Saturday and take communion with a sparkling clean soul. I had not been successful at keeping the sarcasm out of my voice. Her fury was fueled by her own bitter litany:

"A dirty joke, a burden to her family...." She was rolling with her Spanish now, soon the Holy Mother would enter into the picture for good measure. "It's not as if I had not taught you better. Don't you know that those people do not have the example of the Holy Virgin Mary and her Son to follow and that is why they do things for the wrong reasons. Mrs. Nathan said she did not want her son messing around with you—not because of the wrongness of it—but because it would interfere with his studies!" She was yelling now. "She's afraid that he will (she crossed herself at the horror of the thought) make you pregnant!"

"We could say an angel came down and put a baby in my stomach, Mother." She had succeeded in dragging me into her field of hysteria. She grabbed my arm and pulled me to my feet.

"I do not want you associating any more than necessary with people who do not have God, do you hear me?"

"They have a god!" I was screaming now too, trying to get away from her suffocating grasp: "They have an intelligent god who doesn't ask you to believe that a woman can get pregnant without having sex!" That's when she slapped me. She looked horrified at what she had instinctively done.

"Nazi," I screamed, out of control by then too, "I bet you'd like to send Ira and his family to a concentration camp!" At that time I thought that was the harshest thing I could have said to anyone. I was certain that I had sentenced my soul to eternal damnation the minute the words came out of my mouth: but my cheek was burning from the slap and I wanted to hurt her. Father walked into my room at that moment looking shocked at the sight of the two of us entangled in mortal combat.

"Please, please," his voice sounded agonized. I ran to him and he held me in his arms while I cried my heart out on his starched white shirt. My mother, also weeping quietly, tried to walk past us, but he pulled her into the circle. After a few moments, she put her trembling hand on my head.

"We are a family," my father said, "there is only the three of us against the world. Please, please..." But he did not follow the "please" with any suggestions as to what we could do to make things right in a world that was as confusing to my mother as it was to me.

I finished the eighth grade in Paterson, but Ira and I never got together to study again. I sent his Beta Club pin back to him via a mutual friend. Once in a while I saw him in the hall or the playground. But he seemed to be in the clouds, where he belonged. In the fall, I was enrolled at St. Joseph's Catholic High School where everyone believed in the Virgin Birth, and I never had to take a test on the human reproductive system. It was a chapter that was not emphasized.

In 1968, the year Paterson, like many U.S. cities, exploded in racial violence, my father moved us to Augusta, Georgia, where two of his brothers had retired from the army at Fort Gordon. They had convinced him that it was a healthier place to raise teenagers. For me it was a shock to the senses, like moving from one planet to another: where Paterson had concrete to walk on and gray skies, bitter winters and a smorgasbord of an ethnic population; Georgia was red like Mars, and Augusta was green—exploding in colors in more gardens of azaleas and dogwood and magnolia trees—more vegetation than I imagined was possible anywhere not tropical like Puerto Rico. People seem to come in two basic colors: black and blond. And I could barely understand my teachers when they talked in a slowed-down version of English like one of those old 78 speed recordings played at 33. But I was placed in all advanced classes and one of them was biology. This is where I got to see my first real fetal pig which my assigned lab partner had chosen. She picked him up gingerly by the ends of the plastic bag in which it was stored: "Ain't he cute?" she asked. I nodded, nearly fainting from the overwhelming combination of the smell of formaldehyde and my sudden flashback to my brief but intense romance with Ira Nathan.

"What you want to call him?" My partner unwrapped our

specimen on the table, and I surprised myself by my instant recall of Ira's chart. I knew all the parts. In my mind's eye I saw the pencil lines, the labeled photograph. I had had an excellent teacher.

"Let's call him Ira."

"That's a funny name, but OK." My lab partner, a smart girl destined to become my mentor in things Southern, then gave me a conspiratorial wink and pulled out a little perfume atomizer from her purse. She sprayed Ira from snout to tail with it. I noticed this operation was taking place at other tables too. The teacher had conveniently left the room a few minutes before. I was once again stunned—almost literally knocked out by a fist of smell: "What is it?"

"Intimate," my advanced biology partner replied smiling.

And by the time our instructor came back to the room, we were ready to delve into this mystery of muscle and bone; eager to discover the secrets that lie just beyond fear a little past loathing; of acknowledging the corruptibility of the flesh, and our own fascination with the subject.

As I finish packing, the telephone rings and it's my mother. She is reminding me to be ready to visit relatives, to go to a dance with her, and of course, to attend a couple of the services at the church. It is the feast of the Black Virgin, revered patron saint of our home town in Puerto Rico. I agree to everything, and find myself anticipating the eclectic itinerary. Why not allow Evolution and Eve, Biology and the Virgin Birth? Why not take a vacation from logic? I will not be away for too long, will not let myself be tempted to remain in the sealed garden of blind faith; I'll stay just long enough to rest myself from the exhausting enterprise of leading the examined life.

Judith Ortiz Cofer is the author of a novel; a collection of personal essays and poems, *Silent Dancing*, which won a PEN American Citation for the best non-fiction book in 1991; and two poetry collections.

THE FEAR-OF-TOADSTOOLS LADY
/ *James Solheim*

Amanita, blewit, corpse finder—
Because there's so much death out there,
I never go outside. Step on a destroying angel
And you track death right into the house,
Where it dries to a dust that blows
Everywhere in the ventilation, and next
You're breathing poison every day. God,
How terrifying to find a dead man's fingers
On the backyard tree trunk, a dirty trich
By the sandbox, a death cap in the junipers,
A devil's egg in the potato patch.
And they're so sudden!—everywhere
They wait beneath us, the true toadstool
A stringy body underground, much bigger
Than the fruit, the part we see—which
Springs up in a single night of rain.
In the morning they're just there—
Elf cup, false morel, stinky squid—
Like death threats thrown from midnight limousines.
These erections of the underworld—
That's what they are, so cold
And damp—grisette, hygrophoropsis,
Imperial cat—we'll never tame them, never
Stop them from erupting in our lawns like horrid
Jack-in-the-boxes. Jack-o'-lanterns live
In the woods near my house—some nights
I stand in the window and watch them glow.
I even avoid kurotake and morel—
I've read the research. They have toxins too.
I wash everything that comes in the house
Because I know air's full of dust
From liberty cap and nidularia, and I know
The old man of the woods wants to seduce
My children with his poison pie.
I'm inclined to self-instruct
The children, keep them home,

Away from quivering fungus and rhizopogon,
But my husband thinks they need
To learn to live. He says life means
A little danger. I let them out
But when they return I wash the turkey-tail
From their eyelids, the devil's urn
From their lunchpails. Man's split the atom
But hasn't tamed the variegated mop,
Which tells me nature is a chain reaction
Much worse than the ones that man has made.
Any grove could fester quite invisibly
With witches' hats, witches' butter,
Wolf's-milk slime, xylaria—
Giving off a mushroom cloud worth fearing.
I'm happy, though—don't think my staying in
Is fear. I just believe it's sensible
To step on no unruly earth, to risk
No sudden sexual (or asexual) spurt
Of yellow tuning fork or Zeller's bolete.
I like right angles, good corners I can clean,
The cold flat plane of window glass.
Someday I'll go out, when I feel
Like risking something—and oh, what
    drunken intensity
Of living I'll feel then—inhaling panthers,
Pigs' ears, hens of the woods—surviving
To tell of my new life, lungs awhirl
With sweet knot dust. I'll dance
And dance, blooming with spores, till the day
My body's claimed by corpse finders.

ON THE LOGIC AND RADIATION
OF OUR LOVE / *James Solheim*

1.

Venus casts a visible shadow, magnitude -4.4,
On the earthworm with its hundred hearts.
I say this because the worm has a hundred brains,
Except its brains are only ganglia, its main brain's function
To stop the worm, the worm just a muscle
Flinching in the wet grass when the flashlight strikes.
And the heart is a muscle, so the earthworm
Is the heart. Which is why I fear the worms.
They are as automatic as the reason I have not died.

2.

Science has not determined why, in rain, earthworms
    volunteer
Suicidally unto their hell. The hell of earthworms
Is our sidewalks, and their gods are cockeyed flying
    monsters.
There is only one earthworm, because
Their ecstasies are identical; therefore they are immortal.
Yet they have no heaven, because all they have is earth,
And human kings have proven: earth is no heaven.
Yet I'm glad I'm no earthworm, glad I'm not the solution
To problems worms solve. I believe I am more than the
    worm
In my mouth, its quick pink exhortations.

3.

Their goddess is Aphrodite, doubly. Their hearts are
    pure.
Their marriages are eternal, and nights they rise
For her weak light, offering her their tongues: themselves.

Our sun's violence drives them underground.
They bring leaves down point-first for food, run mazes,
Or rise together onto Holland's roofs—the only time
That they suspect the existence of a heaven
Behind our painted moon. Since there are no meditative
  worms,
They can be tricked to the surface with electricity
Or a fork's vibrations. They actually have ten hearts.

4.

You go out with a flashlight, and you grab quick,
On your knees, and knot them around your fingers
To prevent their slick escape. Pull slow. For them you'll
  listen,
Your knees wet like worms, if you desire bass.
The Maori reserved a meal of earthworms for their kings,
Or a lesser man's last meal—but fish got all the worms
  they wanted.
A fish is worms, and worse, so we are worms, and
  worse.
Since love increases heat, love's an infrared of worms.
Often when the earth revolves, stranding us in its
  shadow,
We give off the only radiation our bodies recognize.

5.

No dirty joke, worm husbandry's a science. I'm not a
  worm.
But birth, death, sex—all things that scare me—
Are summarized in worms. Remove all things but worms,
  remove
The earth itself, and everything would still
Be recognizable in its worms (if we include the parasites).
Since worms are sex and worms are death, then sex is
  death,
And since sex causes birth, then death causes birth.
I think I'll join an abbey, renounce the world—

Which, as I've shown, is worms. Purified, de-wormed,
I'll be no body: my only birth the virgin one.

AGAINST BIOGRAPHY / *James Solheim*

I painted because I enjoyed painting.
I stayed unmarried because no one would marry me.
Wearing a sword because swords were in style,
I went out on the morning of my greatest painting
Not even thinking about my father
Breaking into my house to lecture me
Against the excessive use of violet, shouting
So loud he lost the ruins of his last abscessed
And tobacco-reeking tooth. What I did think about
Was simply the rain-sweetened clarity
Of the air, and how clouds like pretentious
Patrons' wives' bouffants balanced
One horizon's timber perfectly. A mantis,
Great claws lifted, crossed the cobbles
Without significance. I picked him up,
Not because my alcoholic father once stabbed
My leg with a broken-off buttonhook, and once
Made me drink vinegar for no reason but spite,
But because people examine strange bugs.
I also saw seven deer, and a caterpillar.
Most days I just painted. Though the other artists
Of my period painted wretchedly, I usually
Said nothing, allowing them their mistakes.
My art forced no artificial meaning on the riot
In the rotten bark, in the fly's corpse
Sucked as hollow as a tooth. If nature's cruelty
Fascinated me, it was only because
She was indeed cruel, and I wanted to paint
Things as they were. Paint is a superior sort
Of fiction—it can describe without commentary.
As Victor Hugo said, fiction lies against fact
While biography lies against significance;
I prefer lies of fact. Biographers love
Not truth, but the grandeur of their own designs.

RETURN OF THE FEAR-OF-TOADSTOOLS LADY
/ *James Solheim*

Out enjoying the town—just walked three miles
Through Jones's woods. Look—on my shoes: mud!
I'm so proud of these grubby hands—I want
To show everyone. And in my bag—three dozen
Morels! (Already checked for bugs,
Dirt knocked off, field guide rules
All followed.) I think I'm flying, Sally,
My world now full of angels' wings and red
Tree brains, chanterelles and earthstars.
The doctor gave me pills. Smell that
Carbon monoxide, that aerosol lead,
The smoke from the tape factory—all
Those risky flavors I'd forgotten.
I feel as if I've moved to a new country,
The town's so big and strange compared to a room.
And it's changed in the ten years
Since I dared risk air full of spores
Of eyelash cup, fuzzy foot, and gypsy.
The Li'l Duffer's gone—too bad—I wanted so much
To eat there again. But now I know
What a mind can do, the poisons
It can save me from—how it stops the fly agaric
(Which is really bloody spit from the horse
Of Wotan as he fled from devils),
The ink coprinus, the jack-o'-lantern, all
The potions boiling in the devil's urn.
You can think a poison right out your pores
If it's not too strong. The powers
Of helvella can't stop me now—from gathering
What I can of earth, from taking
Everything in! If therapy goes well, you
Might see me chasing truffles, or
Maybe I'll come home with a big ziplock
Of toadstools to fry with onions
(It's a test for poison—if the onions
Stay white [or is it if they turn brown?]

They're safe). Life is life, Sally.
I want to drink it all, feel the heady chemistry
Of risk, stroke the skink, then lick
The dirt on my palm for its skinky flavor.
I still believe in God, despite the color
Of storebought agarics, which is identical
To that of the destroying angel.
Sweet knot, lawyer's wig, moose antlers, nidularia—
In my prison I'd forgotten the ways of light.
Therefore I shall kiss the toad on his stool, tempt
The rattler, make it with Carl
In a field of great velvet rider rings.
I'm talking an awful lot, Sally—must be a whiff
Of psilocybe in the breeze. Maybe someday
I'll touch my tongue to one, a psilocybe—just a touch.
Or drink a beer. But probably not.
I even trespassed today, bending barbed wire
Full of tetanus under a hedgeball tree
And some questionable stropharia, right next
To a big TRESPASSERS WILL BE PROSECUTED.
I found a rabid dog there, Sally, and
It chased me, the ground covered with
(I believe) hart truffles. Witches' saliva
Which first grew, in ancient times, from the drool
Of frenzied witches, got all over my soles.
But I did not fall, for God protected me.
Soon I'll see orange peels, rabbit ears, swamp beacons,
Velvet fairy fans; I'll breathe without fear—
In fact, breathe with relish—spores of
Xylaria, yellow pholiota and zoned phlebia.
I will, I swear. By God, I'll eat a sandwich
With my bare hands. I'll kneel on a rock,
Bless myself without counting blessings.
I'll dream the imperial cat, make
The giant puffball my holy grail.
Never again will I fear the devil's bread.

James Solheim teaches at Southern Illinois University. His work has appeared in *The Iowa Review*, *Kenyon Review* and elsewhere.

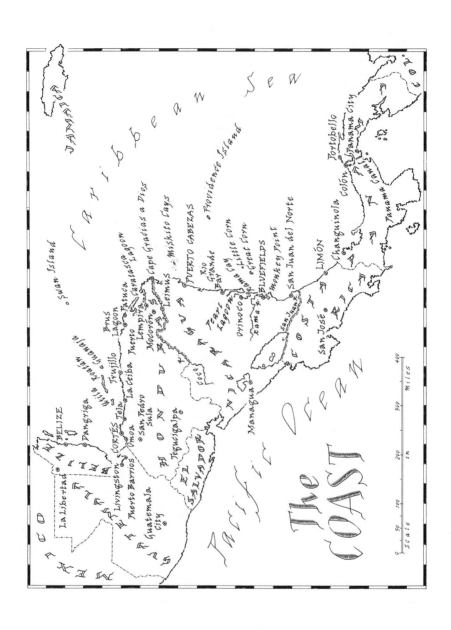

From **AROUND THE EDGE** / *Peter Ford*

In 1988 Peter Ford, an English journalist, decided to travel the Caribbean coast of Central America. Ford began in Belize and journeyed south, by boat and on foot, through Guatemala, Honduras, Nicaragua and Costa Rica, until he reached Panama; there his trip was cut short by Panamanian officials. Ford's upcoming book, *Around the Edge*, chronicles the trip and includes interesting anecdotes and descriptions of the region, as well as information about its history. The following excerpt describes the resistance Ford encountered from Sandinista officials when he attempted to enter Nicaragua, and recounts the first part of his trip down the Coco River in the company of Indian guerillas.

PUERTO LEMPIRA WAS NAMED after a heroic Indian chief, whose noble features glare proudly from Honduran banknotes, but there was nothing noble or heroic about the sweaty, sullen town skulking on the edge of the Caratasca lagoon. A few low municipal buildings of breezeblock and corrugated iron elevated Lempira from the status of village to regional capital of the Honduran Mosquitia. Its potholed roads were covered with gravel, but such pretensions could not disguise the town's self-conscious embarrassment at lying at the end of the world.

Its inhabitants all had the air of being up to no good, sidling suspiciously about their business with mistrustful looks on their faces, and the hot stagnant air, unmoved by a breath of wind, was heavy with intrigue. This was the headquarters of the Eastern front of the U.S. Central Intelligence Agency's war against the Sandinistas.

The local CIA man's home was pointed out to me. Known as Chuck Norris to townspeople scornful of his self-importance but impressed by his helicopter, he lived in the middle of the dusty parade ground of the Honduran army barracks. There, surrounded by open space across which no one could creep without being detected, sat a ship's container, painted a dull red with a line of once significant code letters stencilled in white. At one end of this squat box an entrance had been cut out with a blowtorch, and filled with a heavy metal door. Onto one side an air conditioning unit had been bolted. In that windowless tomb, certain of his security, lived the luckless American charged with organizing the Miskitos into an effective armed struggle against Managua.

One way or another the Miskitos had been waging war on the Sandinista government since 1982, fighting what many of them saw as merely a renewal of their people's historic hostilities with the "Spaniards," using American rather than British guns. Because while the Somoza family that ruled Nicaragua for forty years had been content to leave the coast alone and let its Indians get on with their isolated lives, the Sandinista authorities had stormed into the area in 1979 full of revolutionary fervor and plans to incorporate the coast into the new Nicaragua.

This was not welcomed by a people who hankered for their British colonial past, believed strongly in the conservative precepts of the Moravian church, and never trusted anyone from Managua. Nor did the Sandinistas' passion for land reform and agricultural cooperatives have the slightest relevance to traditional Miskito systems of land tenure. The government's efforts to bring doctors and teachers to the coast did not earn any praise either. Many of them were Cubans, from Fidel Castro's hated communist stronghold, against which the Bay of Pigs invasion had been launched from this very coast; and even if these socialist missionaries were well intentioned, their comrades setting up the state security service were not.

Nothing could endear the Sandinistas to their unwilling citizens, not even the creation of their own organization, which the government had thought might help. Three young Miskitos with secondary education, ambitious and articulate, were put in charge of MISURASATA, which stood for "Miskitos, Sumus, Ramas and Sandinistas Asla Takanka," or "working together." They didn't work together for very long. While Brooklyn Rivera, Steadman Fagoth, and Hazel Lau got down to working out an autonomy charter for the Caribbean coast, the Sandinistas began worrying that the Indians were going to secede. On the coast itself, mutual incomprehension between the people and their new masters was growing dangerously intense, and in early 1981, when the MISURASATA leaders began looking up old maps to see where the borders of the Miskito kingdom had been drawn, and what the British protectorate had looked like, the Sandinistas threw them into jail.

Scarcely had they been freed, after an outcry on the coast, than Steadman Fagoth made a beeline for Honduras, where he had heard that the Americans were secretly organizing an anti-Sandinista guerrilla army. Brooklyn Rivera, slightly more wary of the former Somoza guardsmen who made up the core of that army, went south to Costa Rica. Hazel Lau was talked into cooperating with the Sandinistas.

War broke out in earnest in 1982 when Sandinista troops, enraged by the hit-and-run attacks that Fagoth's men launched from Honduras across the River Coco, resorted to the brutal strategy of razing the earth that is the conventional army's wisdom in the face of guerrilla insurgency. Government soldiers swept down the Coco burning villages, killing cattle, hacking down fruit trees and trampling crops. Twenty thousand Miskitos fled from this rampage, scrambling to the opposite bank of the river and becoming refugees. Another ten thousand, not forewarned in time, were trucked fifty miles south and herded into relocation camps that the Sandinistas had christened Tasba Pri, "free homeland" in Miskito.

The CIA, at that time in the process of creating the "contras," was handed a golden opportunity. An entire people, living along several hundred miles of the Sandinistas' poorly defended eastern flank, in ideal country for guerrilla warfare, had become the government's sworn enemy. The flood of refugees provided a ready pool of young men eager to take up arms. The Honduran government was ready to let them organize and train on the pine-studded plains north of the Coco and to seek refuge there after sorties into Nicaragua.

The opportunity was lost. Over six years of bribes and threats and pressure and manipulation, CIA operatives were never able to overcome the violent rivalry between Rivera and Fagoth, nor create a credible leader who would do Washington's bidding, nor put many more than a thousand men into the field at any one time. For it was not long before it dawned on even the slowest-witted Miskito footsoldier that the United States knew little and cared less about Indian rights in the Mosquitia, and was interested in the Miskitos only as pawns in their greater battle against Managua.

By 1985 the government had had plenty of time to rue the results of its cruel and disastrous policy towards the coast, and more importantly had wrenched itself away from the Latin American left's tradition of regarding all problems with ethnic minorities as a question of class. The Sandinistas concluded that the coast could be quieted only with political concessions, and set about drafting their own autonomy statute for the region. Meanwhile they began cease-fire negotiations with individual guerrilla field commanders, letting them keep their guns and stay in place if they promised to stop attacking the Sandinista army. Unit by unit the government neutralized the military threat, and in 1987 unveiled a plan that gave the Miskitos, Sumus, Ramas and blacks limited but significant control of their political and economic affairs.

By the time I arrived in Puerto Lempira an uneasy temporary truce had been declared the length of the coast, leaving YATAMA, as the anti-Sandinista guerrillas were known, in control of the lower Coco River and a large stretch of country running south from the border. To travel in that area I needed permission from YATAMA, and in Puerto Lempira I hoped to find someone of sufficient authority to issue me with a *laissez-passer*.

I had been given a rough address and a *nom de guerre*; I was looking for "Tigre 17," who could be found three blocks west and one block south of the Moravian mission school.

I found five decrepit houses on that block set back from the street in a patch of rough grass. In the flaccid empty hours of mid-Sunday afternoon the shutters on all the houses were closed. Nothing moved. I strolled up the street trying to look nonchalant, eyeing the houses as I went and wondering which was most likely to be home to a Miskito guerrilla commander and his family.

As I reached the corner and turned to walk round the block two dark-skinned youths ambled towards me, their arms around each others' shoulders. They wore grubby tee-shirts and old jeans, but their feet gave the lie to these civilian clothes. Both boys wore U.S. army issue combat boots: heavy, thick soled, black leather jobs that all the YATAMA fighters used. I asked them which house "the Nicaraguans" lived in.

"Nicaraguans in Puerto Lempira?" one of them asked with faked surprise. "All the Nicaraguans are in the refugee camp in Mocoron."

That was the official line; the Honduran government denied vigorously at every opportunity that it allowed Nicaraguan guerrillas to operate from its territory, but it was scarcely a secret that Lempira was teeming with YATAMA troops who could do as they liked so long as they kept their weapons out of sight. I dropped my voice to a conspiratorial whisper.

"I'm from the agency. I have a message for *el Tigre*."

The teenage soldiers pointed to one of the dilapidated huts I had just walked past. I retraced my steps and called softly to announce my presence. After a moment an unseen hand twitched aside the cotton sheet that was hanging in the doorway and a woman's face appeared. I told her who I was looking for; she frowned and withdrew. From inside the house I heard agitated whispers. The woman poked her head back out again and asked who I was. I told her my name and said I had been sent by

Comandante Blas, the YATAMA military operations chief. I hadn't seen Blas in a couple of years, but I knew he was the most widely respected of the military commanders across a broad spectrum of feuding warlords. His seemed the safest name to drop.

More whispering followed, until I was beckoned in surreptitiously. I stepped into the darkness of the hut and could feel several pairs of eyes on me as my own grew accustomed to the shadows. The inspection felt curious rather than hostile, though, and as soon as I could make out something other than silhouettes in the gloom my heart leaped with surprise and relief; sitting on the bed was a man I recognized, a bear-like *comandante* I had interviewed a year or so earlier. Raul Tobias remembered me too, with an enormous grin. His hefty handshake was open and warm, and as he introduced me to his colleagues as *"mi amigo periodista"* everyone relaxed. Nobody opened the shutters, though.

When I explained what I was doing and that I needed a *permiso* to travel freely through YATAMA controlled territory, Raul insisted that the man I ought to talk to was Wycliffe Diego, a man whose God-fearing parents had christened him after the medieval Bible translator and who himself had taken to the cloth as a Moravian pastor before the Americans had made him YATAMA's political leader.

The CIA had picked Diego primarily because as a pastor he commanded respect from Miskito civilians and was internationally palatable when he was needed to lobby Congress in Washington, and because he was submissive. But his authority over military commanders in the field—the men whose help I would be counting on inside Nicaragua—was minimal. But none of the YATAMA high command were in town, Raul told me, and Wycliffe was. He would take me to see him.

I found him that evening in a small plywood-walled hotel room bare of any furniture but a bed and a stool, and he was only too happy to help me. Since all the lights had gone out in the hotel, and he didn't have a table at which to write, we went across the road to a bar, and there he composed my permit.

"Naha waitna na, witin periodista kum sa England country ba wina," it began. Whether anyone to whom it was addressed would pay any attention I had no idea, but at least it would reassure any suspicious and nervous guerrillas I might come across that I was known to their leader. I hoped.

That Monday morning at the U.N. camp in Mocoron I found the administrative building besieged by refugees waiting to hear their name called out by the brisk young woman from the capital who was distributing money. Tomorrow these families would be returning to Nicaragua, and if they faced an uncertain future, so many years of homelessness and a life without purpose had finally numbed them to the hazards they were about to confront.

Inside, in the thatched and shuttered cool of the office of the local representative of the U.N. High Commissioner for Refugees, a sense of order prevailed. The Frenchman in charge, with the eyes of a spaniel accustomed to regular beatings, quite understood that I wanted to cross the border, and why, and when and how, and would be perfectly happy to put me on a truck tomorrow with the refugees. Except that he did not have the authority to do so. Only the Colonel, he told me regretfully, could permit such a passage across the frontier.

It was clear from the manner in which he referred to the Colonel that the Frenchman had suffered only arbitrary injustice and humiliation at his hands, and that I could expect nothing else myself. The Colonel, head of the Fifth Battalion of the Honduran army and the local military authority, liked to call himself the new King of the Miskitos, I was told, for the power he wielded in his autonomous fiefdom. He also enjoyed a reputation for liking to make other people's lives miserable.

I said that in that case I had better ask the Colonel's permission to accompany the refugees the next morning. The Frenchman looked mournful. He had himself been hoping to talk to the Colonel for three days but had not succeeded in securing an audience. I was welcome to try. And if I did manage to see him, would I mind passing on the message that the UNHCR chief would like a word?

I walked the three miles down the gravel track through the pine forest that led to the Fifth Battalion headquarters until I came to a brightly painted red and white striped wooden pole stretched across the road. A pair of suspicious eyes peered at me through the gun slit in the sandbagged sentry post. I explained that I had come to see the Colonel and could I kindly pass. The eyes did not change their expression but I heard a snigger. I hesitated. Sometimes, I had found in dealing with half-witted Honduran soldiers, it was worth adopting a tone of authority, hoping they would respond to that, rather than to the sight of a scruffy foreign journalist. The snigger, however, did not suggest a half-wit. It sounded more as if the Colonel had instilled his taste for arbitrary power into even his lowliest sentry. I decided to be polite.

An explanation of who I was and what I wanted elicited only a hand stretched through the gunslit and a curt order. *"Pasaporte."* I complied, and heard the sentry crank up his field telephone. "Post number one to the Colonel's office," I heard him shout. "Request for audience with the Colonel. Ford, Peter. British. Journalist." He waited for a response. Outside the sentry box, under the sun, feeling very alone in the emptiness, I waited for a response. It arrived, a throaty crackle over the primitive phone line. The hand reappeared, proffering my passport. I took it. The eyes reappeared. "Request refused."

It was spoken so definitively that further enquiry seemed futile, but I could scarcely leave it at that. Could I perhaps return at an hour more convenient to the Colonel. "I don't know." Could he ring the Colonel's office again to find out? "No." Was I unable to see the Colonel because he had refused to see me or merely because he was not there at the moment? "I don't know." Could he ring the Colonel's office again to find out? Even as I asked I guessed the response. Out of principle rather than hope I wrote a note addressed to the Colonel explaining who I was and what I wanted from him, and pushed it through the gunslit, asking that my message be passed on. The sentry just grunted.

For the next four days I laid siege to the Colonel, dogging his imagined footsteps, pouncing on every jeep that emerged from his headquarters from dawn to dusk one day and never setting eyes on him. I had lost the chance of crossing the border on the day I had appointed with the Sandinistas, and very possibly I had lost the chance of crossing altogether. As I lay on my bed between sorties, suffocating in the cell that Don Charlie, a baggy-faced Chinaman and owner of Mocoron's sole restaurant, had rented to me, my goal of reaching Nicaragua developed into a monstrous obsession, fed by my mute, helpless fury at being so capriciously frustrated.

I learned from a UNHCR official who had spoken to the Colonel's deputy that he had definitely received the note I had left for him. He knew I was in Mocoron, he knew I was desperate to get out, he knew he was the only person who could authorize my departure and he was being very careful to do nothing that might be construed as helpful. He was not avoiding me; it would have been beneath his dignity to go out of his way to avoid a struggling Englishman in need of his favor. But he was confident that his movements were sufficiently unpredictable, his subordinates sufficiently secretive and his means of transport sufficiently varied (one day he flew to Tegucigalpa by helicopter from his army base, thwarting the guard I had mounted on the refugee camp airstrip) to make him well nigh impossible to track down.

Until Thursday morning, as I sat outside my room watching Don Charlie's mongrel dog worrying at a tired old sow that lay in the dust of the yard, Charlie emerged from his kitchen, threw a stone at his dog, and told me casually that he had seen the Colonel driving towards the army post by the landing strip.

I bounded out of the yard and raced the five hundred yards to the airstrip. Bumping towards me up the track from the army post came an open-topped jeep. I stood in the middle of the path and the jeep pulled up. At the end of the gravelled landing strip, shimmering away into the distance, we were alone. At the wheel sat a dour flat-faced man in mirror aviator shades and camouflage fatigues. No rank insignia or name patch indicated his identity.

"I'm looking for the Colonel."

"Why?"

"To ask him for a permit." The driver looked at me impassively and left his engine running but he shifted the gear into neutral. *He was going to listen to me.*

"To do what?"

"To cross the border with the refugees at Leimus."

"There's no customs post here. Foreigners are obliged to go through customs." My mouth went dry.

"*Migracion* in Tegucigalpa gave me preliminary permission." I showed him the scribbled authorization I had secured in the capital after so much cajoling. "But they said the final decision would be the Colonel's."

He grunted. He clearly liked his butter laid on even thicker.

This was my only chance to continue my journey, I pleaded. The book I planned to write depended on his magnanimity. I grovelled. He was the only man who could help me. I beseeched.

I had leaned one hand against the bonnet of the jeep. It seemed too familiar. I removed it and shifted to a more respectful stance, my hands behind my back. That was too abjectly schoolboyish. I folded my arms across my chest. The Colonel merely stared silently from behind his sunglasses, revelling in my discomfort. On one of his fleshy fingers resting on the steering wheel a large purple stone set in a bulky bronze graduation ring caught the sun. He pushed his forage cap back. "You need a UNHCR permit," he parried.

"I have it." I handed him the letter that the UNHCR chief in Tegucigalpa had written for me. He grunted again.

"But they know they have to send a note to the Armed Forces Public Relations office and they have to give their permission for this."

"At the Public Relations office they said the decision was yours," I insisted.

"Who told you that?"

"The people in the office," I said lamely. I hadn't actually visited the PR office and it seemed wise to be as vague as possible.

He shifted one booted foot onto the jeep's running board and stared at me. I stared at my reflection in his sunglasses.

"When would this border crossing take place?"

I'm winning.

"As soon as possible. There's a special repatriation tomorrow morning at seven thirty."

"But I have an office and it's not here."

"If you did give me permission, a UNHCR driver has told me he could pick it up from your headquarters this evening," I pressed.

He snorted, but not a muscle moved in his face. He asked for my full name. I handed him my passport and he read it. "Give the permit to Lieutenant Ballesteros at the frontier." He put his jeep back into gear and drove away. He had never told me directly that he would give me a permit. He had never actually acknowledged that he was the Colonel. But that night, my permit was duly written, stamped, signed and sealed. I would be allowed out of Honduras. Would I be allowed into Nicaragua?

The returning refugees were beginning their lives again with pitifully little. One boastful fool had spent his family's repatriation money on a showy radio-cassette player, and was playing it loudly for all to hear. When the batteries he had bought ran out he would have no more use for his expensive toy: batteries were all but unobtainable in Nicaragua. Most had been more cautious, settling for new clothes, Wellington boots, kerosene lamps and sacks of vegetables as their defense against uncertainty.

The refugees who were staying behind, still too wary of the Sandinistas' promises to risk another trauma, stood around the six trucks looking skeptical, stretching out their hands uncertainly for a farewell clasp as one by one the engines choked into life. On board, the atmosphere was charged with noisy excitement. Never had I seen a group of Miskitos in such a good mood. When the convoy stopped at a military checkpoint on a rise, we all looked out over the pine tops into the gray distance. "That's Nicaragua," someone said, and the truck fell silent for a moment as everybody stared.

The Coco is a sacred river to the Miskitos, especially to those who live along its shores, a focus of their culture and a unifying myth signifying plenty. Only on maps is it a dividing line, spelled out as the frontier adjudicated by the International Court of Justice at The Hague on November 18th, 1960. When we arrived a torrential rain was whipping the muddy current into a froth and shrouding the far side from view, but that was the least of my troubles once I had had a word with the UNHCR official from the Nicaraguan side and heard him tell me that I could not cross with the refugees in the giant canoes (although I could pay a boatman later if I liked), that he would not give me a ride to Puerto Cabezas, that as far as he was concerned I had no right to be there and that he had had too many "tourists" entering Nicaragua like this.

An arrogant, beaky-nosed sneering Spaniard who insisted on speaking to me in his pitiful English under the impression that he spoke it fluently, Jorge Delamotta had an extremely high opinion of himself. In his egocentric imagination he had sloughed off his identity as a lowly bureaucrat trying to organize five canoes in the rain in the back of beyond, and had become singlehandedly responsible for the resettlement of the entire Miskito people. This was tiresome, but there was nothing to be done about it but be patient. I sat under a dripping tree and watched him sliding around in the mud dispatching his canoes until the last one was about to leave, half-empty, when I suggested in as reasonable a voice as I could muster that I would not be causing him any difficulties if I jumped on too. He relented.

My appearance at the end of a queue of Miskito Indians filling in their entry forms in the chaotic gloom of the Nicaraguan customs post clearly struck the immigration officer behind his counter as irregular. And if there is one thing that a low-ranking Sandinista official disliked, it was an irregularity that might call for some initiative to be taken. Lt. Ricardo Zuniga knew what to do with irregularities: send them back where they came from.

All my efforts to alert the Sandinista authorities to my plans had been in vain. Lt. Zuniga had never heard of me. No, he had not been expecting me last Tuesday, no, he had no orders to let me pass, no, foreigners were not authorized to enter Nicaragua here, especially when they had no Honduran exit stamp in their passports as I did not, no no no no no.

He had not even deigned to look at the letter that I was intending to use to open every official door on the coast in Nicaragua, a letter of support from the top two Sandinista officials in the region. I had been given it just before leaving Managua three months earlier and I had been counting on it as a passe-partout in an area where normally every foreign visitor was obliged to register his every step a week in advance.

Dated March 2nd and addressed to my name, *Comandante Guerrillero* Lumberto Cambell, the top Sandinista at the Southern end of the coast, and *Sub-Comandante* Jose Gonzalez, the boss in Puerto Cabezas, announced that they "support your project of writing a book about the Atlantic Coast of Central America and do not doubt that the results of same will be important study material for our work."

"Before entering Nicaraguan territory it would be helpful if you could inform us of the date and of the route you intend to follow in order that we can issue the appropriate instructions to facilitate your mission."

I forced Lt. Zuniga to read this missive and looked at him triumphantly. He could scarcely turn me back if I had Cambell's and Gonzalez' blessing.

"But you didn't inform anyone of the date you were coming," he said truculently.

"Oh, yes I did. My wife told the Interior Ministry in Managua that I would be arriving last Tuesday, and when I was delayed I sent a note with the UNHCR officials for Sub-Comandante Gonzalez telling him I would be coming over later in the week."

"Well we didn't hear anything. And anyway, it's expired."

"What's expired?"

"This letter. It's dated March 2nd. That's nearly three months ago."

In vain I tried to explain that this was not a permit valid for a certain length of time; it was a letter written on the eve of my departure from Managua and its contents did not go stale over time like the corn tortilla that Lt. Zuniga was chewing on as he heard me out. My arrival was all highly irregular and that was all there was to it.

But he did not appear eager to send me back into Honduras, at least not immediately, so I thought it better not to force the issue until I had come up with some more arguments. I was trapped in a no-man's-land on the frontier and in the no-man's-land of Lt. Zuniga's indecision as he wrestled to match my unexpected and troublesome presence to the rules and regulations he lived by. It was the meticulous care with which I saw him inspecting each of the 245 immigration forms the refugees had filled in that suggested an argument that might make sense to him.

I sidled back up to the counter. "If you won't let me into Nicaragua," I asked innocently, "what do you suggest I do?"

"We could find you a boat across the river," he told me.

"Back into Honduras?"

"Yes."

"But the Honduran authorities on the other side are only there for the refugees and they are only allowed to let people out of the country, not into it," I said.

"Really?"

"And that means that they don't have any entry forms at their immigration post. I couldn't possibly get past them."

That clinched it as far as Lt. Zuniga was concerned. If the Hondurans didn't have the right forms then there was no point at all in sending me back. I would have to come into Nicaragua, but he would have to talk to his superiors in Puerto Cabezas to ask for further instructions.

That was all I wanted. In Puerto Cabezas, I was confident, Chepe Gonzalez would be able to sort everything out. But Lt. Zuniga's radio was out of action and Jorge Delamotta said he could not possibly allow anyone other than UNHCR personnel to use the radio in his jeep.

Up until then their common reluctance to let me pass had made allies of Delamotta and Zuniga, but now that the Lieutenant had decided I could not go back to Honduras he began to see my presence as an opportunity rather than a problem. If I had to go to Puerto Cabezas I also had to be accompanied. For Lt. Zuniga Puerto Cabezas was home, and a great deal more attractive than the woebegone rain-sodden customs post he was stationed at. His indecision vanished.

"You are being detained," he told me. "You will be taken under escort to Puerto Cabezas." I almost held out my hands to be cuffed, I was so glad to be arrested. Lt. Zuniga did not feel such dramatic gestures were called for, but he did unholster his pistol and keep it on his lap as we jolted down the track. He kept his weapon at the ready not for my benefit, I found, but from fear of ambush, as we drove past a gutted military transport rusting in the ditch. Too many government vehicles had been set upon on this lonely road by Miskito guerrillas, and Lt. Zuniga had little faith in the truce that had recently been declared.

Nor did Sub-Lieutenant Mario, who ran the Interior Ministry post at La Tronquera where we halted to radio Puerto Cabezas. Installed as the chief of internal security in this remote village full of surly Miskitos who talked behind his back in a language he didn't understand, the Sub-Lieutenant had surrounded himself with the familiar and reassuring symbols of the revolution he served. Hung on the walls of his clapboard office as he sat behind a monstrous and ancient typewriter and a pile of snub-nosed M-79 shells were an AK-47 assault rifle, a bunch of olive drab knapsacks and ammunition belts and a banner in the red and black colors of the Sandinista Front depicting a youth brandishing a book in one hand and a rifle in the other. Below a photograph of the nine supreme Sandinista *comandantes* he had copied out the three cardinal rules that succored him in the long nights of uncertainty as to whether enemy assassins were prowling outside his window:

"Philosophers have only interpreted the world in various ways. The point is to change it." Karl Marx.

"The great cardinal problem of all philosophy, especially of modern philosophy, is the relationship between thinking and being." F. Engels.

"Marx's doctrine is all powerful because it is exact, complete and ordered, and it gives people a monolithic conception of the world." V.I. Lenin.

When the Sub-Lieutenant had finished informing his superiors in Puerto Cabezas that he had in his charge a loose Englishman with an out-of-date letter, and while we were waiting for instructions, he gravely explained the relationship between being and thinking. How much success was he going to have with the Sandinistas' new "hearts and minds" campaign among the Indians if he went on like this?

It was not long before Puerto Cabezas came back on the radio. I was to be taken to the Immigration Office there immediately for questioning. Silently I rejoiced. In Puerto I should at least be able to find an official with sufficient authority and sense to grant me that letters of introduction did not expire.

Sub-Comandante Julio Rugama, a slim mustachioed young man with canny eyes and four bright brass echelons on the epaulettes of his newly pressed green uniform, had as much authority as anyone in Special Zone I, as Northern Zelaya had become known in Sandinista-speak. He was the senior officer of the Interior Ministry, the Minister's personal delegate, and what he said, went.

He was also the head of the secret police, and he wanted to know what I thought I had been doing, entering the country at an unauthorized border post at a spot adjacent to enemy-held territory.

I apologized, explained, and tendered the oft-folded, torn and rather damp letter that Gonzalez and Cambell had written for me. He agreed that it had not expired. I thanked him. He regretted that warning of my arrival had never been passed to his office. So did I. How did I intend to proceed?

I explained that I planned to return to the Coco River near where I had crossed, and then to follow it downstream to the sea before turning south down the coast and thus back to Puerto, before continuing south towards Bluefields. I wanted his authorization to make the journey.

"I wish I could help you," he said affably, leaning across his desk to offer me a cigarette. "But we don't have a single soldier anywhere you say you are going. Having my written permission would not just be worthless; it would be dangerous. That's all contra territory. What are you going to do about the contras?"

I hesitated. To tell him merely that I would deal with them as and when I found them was not going to wash. He would not let me drive out of Puerto towards rebel-held areas so ill-prepared: he was, after all, nominally responsible for the whole of Special Zone I and felt partially responsible for my safety. On the other hand, to tell the chief of Sandinista security that I'd cleared everything in advance with the enemy and that they had issued me safe conduct passes seemed to be inviting suspicion. I coughed. The Sub-Comandante raised his eyebrows. I could not dissemble.

"Well, yes, I'd thought about that," I conceded. "And, umm, to be on the safe side you see, just in case, I umm, went to talk to one or two of them."

"And what did they tell you?"

Reluctantly, I pulled from my money belt the letter that Wycliffe Diego had written me, and one that the best-known Miskito rebel leader, Brooklyn Rivera, had made out a few months earlier when I had visited him in Costa Rica. I was particularly nervous about showing Rugama the letter from Brooklyn. More than a safe conduct pass, it was a warmly expressed recommendation typed on YATAMA-headed writing paper describing me as "an honest and upright person" and urging "indigenous brothers to give him all support and collaboration" on my journey. He could scarcely have broadcast more clearly my sympathy for the Miskito cause, and I had thanked him for his help when he had drafted the letter. Now, sitting across from the Sub-Comandante as he read through it for a second time, I felt that perhaps I had not been wise to show it to him.

Rugama pushed the piece of paper across the desk towards me and tapped it deliberately with his forefinger. I held my breath.

"With a letter like that in your possession," he said, looking hard into my eyes, "travelling in Nicaragua at a time when U.S.— funded Miskito guerrillas are fighting an undeclared war against the popular Sandinista government..."

He paused. I swallowed.

"...I would say that with this letter you can go anywhere you want on the coast and you won't have any trouble."

He smiled at the way he had taken me aback. "No, really, I mean it. In the places you are going an authorization from Rivera is of much more use than anything I can make out. You are free to go."

In the days of the English, Puerto Cabezas had been known as Bragman's Bluff for the low sandstone cliff that held the town clear of the breakers on the stony beach below, but it was the Americans who had lent the town its fleeting prosperity. Digging gold from the nearby mines of Bonanza, tapping rubber from the jungle, cutting timber from the stands of pine, planting bananas on swampy riverbanks or canning turtle meat from the Cayes offshore, American companies had shipped their booty through Puerto Cabezas from the early years of the twentieth century in continuous cycles of boom and bust.

But by the time I was making my journey there had been no more companies on the coast for the past twenty years. They pulled out when there was no more money to be made, and they left their Miskito workers stranded between the disappearing stern of the last steamer and the remains of a culture they had in large part abandoned.

I went to evensong at the neat little whitewashed Moravian church, a sober wooden structure redeemed from austerity by its red window frames, painted to match the zinc roof and spire.

Inside, its only adornment was an ancient clock whose pendulum marked time with the measured cadence of the Reverend Shogreen's sermon.

The Reverend Andy Shogreen, a moonfaced bespectacled black man, preached in English to his congregation made up mostly of plump matrons squeezed into starched Sunday dresses. It was Mothers' Day, and the Reverend Shogreen did not approve of Mothers' Day. It led men to think that only mothers were responsible for children, whereas the Bible commanded us to honor our mother and our father. Mothers' Day was just another aspect of the double standard on virginity from which women in Puerto Cabezas suffered. This all seemed rather advanced stuff from a conservative Protestant preacher, and I flipped through the Moravian hymnal to see if anything like it could be found in the church's approved texts.

There, in the Litany, I came across a prayer to be used in time of war. "Grant, O Lord, unto the President of the United States, in these times of danger, Thy gracious counsel, that in all things he may approve himself the father of the people."

With the President of the United States funding a war against the Nicaraguan government, the Reverend Shogreen had found this an embarrassing supplication, and an "erratum" slip had been pasted over it to offer a more general prayer that the Lord might "deliver us from the sins that give rise to war." But it could not disguise the fact that as far as most Miskitos were concerned, God was naturally on America's side, and there was not much the Sandinistas could do about that.

I asked the Reverend Shogreen for a letter of introduction to Moravian pastors I might come across in no-man's-land and in YATAMA-controlled areas. The wider the range of safe-conducts I could gather, the more confident I felt. He gave me one, but it was a member of his congregation who offered the most practical piece of advice I had heard on how to handle the next leg of my journey.

It was all very well having permits from both sides in this war to go where I was going, he explained to me when we fell into conversation after the service. But when I came across a patrol in the jungle, how was I to know which army it belonged to? After all, soldiers from both sides carried the same AK-47 assault rifles, and they all mixed and matched their battle fatigues according to what they had pulled off the dead bodies of their enemies, and which style of camouflage they favored. I could get into serious trouble if I ran into the rebels, mistook them for the regular army and produced my letter from Sub-Comandante Gonzalez, he pointed out.

If I came across soldiers, he told me, I should look at their ankles. The rebels, like the American advisers who had trained them, folded their trouser bottoms tightly into their combat boots. Sandinista troops, on the other hand, tucked their trousers loosely into their socks. *"It joss a liddle deetail, mon, bot it de onliest way to tell em apaart."*

I found the village of Koom in YATAMA's hands and as soon as I arrived I had been surrounded by guerrillas who wanted to know who I was and what I was doing there. They were more curious than hostile, though, and their doubts were easily stilled by a packet of American cigarettes, especially when one of them, who introduced himself as Hubert, the local intelligence officer, and took me aside for a few questions, recognized me from a Miskito rebel assembly I had attended in Honduras a couple of years earlier.

The thirty or so teenage soldiers hanging about Koom were enjoying the cease-fire, swaggering around the village parading their weapons before admiring clutches of small children. Some of the guerrillas who had family in Koom were making better use of their time off at home, setting aside their rifles to help clear land or build houses.

Hubert told me bluntly that my hopes of travelling downriver to the coast were unrealistic. There was no traffic, he said, no boats, no engines and no petrol. I mulled this over as I lay in my hammock that night in the Moravian church storeroom while below me mice gnawed their way into sacks of rice seed. If Hubert were right, the only way out of Koom was back the way I had come, when the church truck made its way back to the river. That would quash my main reason for venturing this deep into Nicaragua's northeastern corner: to find the Miskito crown jewels. Historical records speak of crowns and scepters and orbs sent from London to successive Miskito kings at their coronations down the centuries, and though everybody told me that they had been lost long ago if they had ever really existed, it was those myths that had drawn me here.

I was eating the breakfast that the pastor's wife had prepared for me when one of the guerrillas called me from the kitchen to tell me that *el jefe* wanted a word with me. His tone was sufficient to make it clear that *el jefe* was not going to wait for me to finish my rice and beans.

I was brought before a burly man with a dark scowl, hung about with every possible accoutrement of war: a spiderweb of straps and webbing, spare magazines for his AK-47, a pistol, a map case and compass, torch, water bottle and his rifle itself slung behind his shoulder. He did not bother to introduce himself as he asked me who I was.

He shook his head disapprovingly as he read my letter of introduction. "This isn't Wycliffe's signature," he growled in strongly Miskito-accented Spanish. "Who gave you this?"

There was little I could do except assure him that I had had the letter from Wycliffe's own hand and had watched him sign it just a few days earlier at the hotel in Puerto Lempira. *El jefe* remained unconvinced.

"They're all politicos anyway in Lempira, and I'm a *militar*. There's too much trickery amongst the politicos, all they do in Lempira is fuck around with their half-assed maneuvering for power. I take orders from Blas and no one else. No one's told me anything about you."

Blas was YATAMA's military chief of staff whom I had failed to find in Lempira. But if this man took orders only from the chief of staff he had to be pretty senior himself. It occurred to me that he might be Siskar, the rebels' top field commander in the whole area I was hoping to travel through. I asked him cautiously if that was who he was and he nodded. My heart leapt. The Reverend Shogreen had told me he knew Siskar well; triumphantly I pulled from my money belt the letter he had written me, addressed to all community leaders. Siskar shoved it back into my hands without even glancing at it. "I don't want to see anything from a pastor," he snorted.

I suggested that if he didn't believe in my letter of introduction from Diego he should radio his headquarters, and if he didn't mind I would like to go with him, to be able to speak directly to the people in Honduras. I was by no means sure that the radio operator would be able to find Diego or any of his lieutenants, and if headquarters replied that no one there knew anything about me, Siskar might feel inclined to investigate my identity more closely. It would not take him long to find my letters of authority from the Sandinistas and then God only knew what he might decide to do with me.

While Siskar watched me in silence I babbled on nervously about the journey I was making and the contact I had had as a journalist in Honduras with Miskito rebel leaders. I dropped as many names as I could remember from the hurried clandestine meetings in Tegucigalpa that contra spokesmen would call occasionally.

"Have you ever spoken to Brooklyn Rivera?" he asked me suddenly.

That pulled me up short. Rivera's forces, as far as I knew, were concentrated in the south of Nicaragua, closer to his Costa Rican refuge. And the rivalry between Miskito rebel chiefs was often fiercer than their common hatred of the Sandinistas. Siskar was loyal to Wycliffe, who hated Brooklyn, I reasoned, so it would be safer to say I had never met him. But something in Siskar's voice suggested that his question was not a trap. Yes, I acknowledged, I had spoken to Brooklyn. Here was a letter from him.

No sooner had he finished reading it than Siskar plunged into a political discussion. Did I think the cease-fire would last? Did I believe Sandinista troops would really be confined to their barracks? Would the government allow food supplies into rebel-held areas? Were the Sandinistas honestly prepared to recognize Indian rights?

I was circumspect in my opinions, but Siskar clearly welcomed the opportunity to discuss with an outsider the questions he was wrestling with, tempted as he was to come in from six years in the bush but deeply skeptical of the government's proclaimed good faith. At any rate he decided I could be left alone in Koom while he went downriver to his camp to radio headquarters personally "so that we get things straight."

Whom he talked to and what they said I never discovered, but by the time Siskar returned three hours later he was full of apologies for the way he had dealt with me that morning and anxious to help in any way he could. I explained that I was trying to reach Cape Gracias a Dios at the mouth of the Coco.

"I've got the same problem myself," he told me. "The gringos dropped us some supplies downriver yesterday and we need to move them to the coast but I've no way to do it because we've run out of petrol."

He had a boat, he said, and he had an engine, and he knew of a man who had a drum of fuel that nobody but YATAMA had any use for but he didn't have the money to pay for it.

He left the solution hanging in the air, and I reached for it immediately. If his men would carry me down to the Cape in their supply boat, I would buy the petrol to get us there. I was not entirely comfortably offering a little personal humanitarian aid to the *contras* to supplement the $100 million that the U.S. Congress had voted that year, but if that was what it took to get me out of Koom, that was what I would do.

The war was far from everybody's mind as we poled the heavy square nosed *pipante*, hollowed from an enormous tree trunk, away from the steep bank and into the current. The four young guerrillas chosen to accompany me were in high spirits at this unexpected break in their routine and behaved as if they were on a school outing, while the boy at the tiller gunned the outboard engine mercilessly to bring the prow out of the water like a speedboat's. They calmed down a little when a submerged log struck us a glancing blow that nearly overturned the boat, but excitement overtook them again at the sight of a large white goose standing motionless on the sandy shore of a bend in the river. The sergeant in charge of our party, a slight man with a narrow face who had chosen the peculiar *nom de guerre* of Damalupia which meant Old lady, told the tillerman to slow down and took aim with his AK-47. As he fired his shot the bird rose in a puff of feathers, flapped its wings in a few weak beats and dropped into a patch of tall reeds. Hooting with anticipation we beached the canoe and tumbled out in search of the stricken goose. But the reeds were ten feet tall and grew so thickly together that we found nothing more rewarding than bloodstains. That night, when we stopped at a small group of bamboo huts perched above the river where YATAMA troops kept some stores, we had only the guerrillas' basic fare for supper, oatmeal porridge.

The next morning we set off to collect the supplies that we were to carry down to the Cape. A U.S. transport plane had dropped them a day earlier by the river and now they had to be distributed among the YATAMA troops. We reached the drop zone by mid-morning, and it was immediately apparent that something was wrong. There were no neatly piled cartons of stores nor crates of medicine on the riverbank. Instead we found half a dozen sweaty guerrillas up to their knees in swamp, tugging fruitlessly at the corners of sacks stubbornly embedded in the muck.

One of them gave up the task with a stream of foul abuse and explained to me what had happened. It was all, he said, the fault of "Chuck Norris," the CIA man who lived in a shipping container in the middle of the parade ground in Puerto Lempira.

"Chuck" had flown out a couple of weeks earlier in his helicopter in search of a good place to drop the next batch of supplies. His eye had been caught by this wide stretch of flat treeless land right by the river bank, about the size of five football pitches. The drop would happen here, he ruled. The Miskito rebel officer to whom he had communicated this decision had apparently voiced some reservations. He knew this part of the river, he had said, and when it rained, this likely looking drop zone flooded and turned into an enormous marsh.

"Chuck" had apparently been unimpressed. Miskitos, he had told the YATAMA officer, did not know enough about air drops to choose the best places to carry them out. That was his job, and this was an ideal drop zone. The goods would arrive in fifteen days' time. YATAMA should make sure they had enough men on hand to gather them up.

Two weeks later, on the eve of the drop, it had rained heavily. Five planes had flown the supply mission, each laden with several tons of food and other essential goods. One by one they had passed over the drop zone and with practiced accuracy offloaded their cargo just where they had been told to. Straight into the swamp. Three months' food supplies for a thousand men were lost or ruined. More than fifteen tons of beans, sugar, rice, lard, oatmeal and soap, and only the soap could be salvaged. When a 100 lb. sack of beans is dropped onto dry ground from 1,000 feet without a parachute, it leaves a three-foot-deep crater, but at least the beans can be recovered from their split sacks. When the same sack of beans is dropped from that height into a bog it simply disappears.

Nobody seemed to know if the Americans would drop them some replacement supplies once news of the disaster filtered back to Swan Island, the Honduran island halfway to the Caymans where contra logistics were organized. So we loaded onto our *pipante* a few cases of powdered milk that had been left over from a previous drop and headed downstream to the nearest radio set to report the cockup.

Once we had done so, and taken on board a young comandante named Ben, the crew decided to take it easy. With one lad up front waving his AK-47 to left or right to indicate a path through the submerged logs and branches, we followed the looping sweeping bends of the river, stopping now and again at fruit trees to pick some guavas or a wild papaya. At one point we pulled in alongside the bank to visit two soldiers manning a small weapons depot in a forest clearing. Their marksmanship had been better than Damalupia's; on a fire by their tent bubbled a pot of stewing duck. We plunged our fingers in greedily, pulling out chunks of rich, dark meat and wolfing them down. Ben grinned at me as he wiped the grease from his chin with his uniform sleeve. *"Dass life on de Coco, mon. Lil by lil you get you lonch."*

The guerrillas seemed accustomed to disasters such as the wasted supply drop, and used to improvising solutions. Because the flat bottomed *pipante* that had carried us downstream was unstable on the open sea, a small sailing boat had been commandeered to take us and our load of powdered milk across the Cape Gracias a Dios bar, where Columbus had anchored and won the coast, to a YATAMA base at old Cape.

But there was no sailing boat waiting for us. Ben decided to paddle across the river to a settlement on the Honduran bank, to see what had gone wrong, but first he had to change into a red tee shirt and a pair of jeans that he pulled from his pack. The Honduran army maintained an outpost in the settlement, and for appearances' sake, since the contras were officially not meant to be in Honduras, YATAMA troops were expected to wear civilian clothes in the presence of Honduran authorities. Pulling on the jeans seemed a strangely comic act of diplomacy in such a remote and hidden corner of this jungle.

We passed the time waiting for him talking about Nicaragua as if it were a foreign country. "How much would this shirt cost in Nicaragua?" "Can you get trousers like these in Nicaragua?" Sub-Comandante Rugama, the Sandinista chief in Puerto Cabezas, had been right; the central government's writ simply didn't extend this far. The only currency anyone ever saw was the U.S. dollar or the Honduran lempira, all the food and goods that found their way here came from Honduras, not from Nicaragua, and as Damalupia insisted, "First of all we are indigenous Indians and then we are Nicaraguans."

As we lay beneath a tree on the riverbank, brushing ants off our clothes, Damalupia studied closely a ten dollar bill he had asked me to show him. I had rarely looked at more than the denomination of American banknotes; Damalupia pored over the bill intently, insisting on an explanation of everything he saw. No one had any money out here, let alone real American money, and his fascination demanded an exhaustive inspection.

"This note is legal tender for all debts, public and private," I translated into Spanish, skipping over the portrait of Hamilton, of whom I knew little. Damalupia didn't care; his eye had already caught a serious anomaly. The note was signed not only by James A. Baker III, Secretary of the Treasury, but by the Treasurer of the United States, Katherine Davalos Ortega. How could this be? Damalupia demanded. How could a relative of his arch enemy, the evil Nicaraguan President Daniel Ortega, be responsible for the symbol of power and goodness, the U.S. dollar?

The engraving of the U.S. Treasury on the other side of the bill did not engage his attention as much as a few stick figures on the pavement that I had not noticed. "Who are these people?" he wanted to know. "Civilians?" In his world there were just three classes of people: Sandinistas, to be killed; *militares*, his comrades in YATAMA; and civilians. These were civilians, I said. "Going to change their dollars, I suppose," he laughed.

Ben returned with the news that the catboat was nowhere to be seen and that we would have to march three hours to Old Cape. We had already suspected as much, and the men greeted the order to load the powdered milk onto their backs with groans of resignation.

Through thickening darkness we pushed our way along a scarcely visible forest path, branches whipping into my eyes and catching on my pack, coarse sharp grasses cutting at my hands. When Ben led the way out of the wood onto a beach I cheered under my breath—the afternoon's good-natured chatter had subsided into dogged silence during the march—but underfoot I found not the sand of a beach but the squelch of a mudflat. The mudflat quickly turned into a lagoon but we plodded single file through the dusk and the shin deep water regardless, disturbing stingrays that roiled up the shallows at our approach, their tails leaving an elegant single ripple as their wake in the black water.

We arrived at the base to find there was no food beyond a mugful each of oatmeal and water, flavored with sugar. I forced it down and fell into my hammock, asleep before the mosquitos found me.

Peter Ford is an English journalist who lived and worked in Latin America for six years. He is currently Middle East correspondent for the *Christian Science Monitor*.

Thomas Sanchez

© Rollie McKenna

Thomas Sanchez has written three novels, *Mile Zero*, *Rabbit Boss*, and *Zoot-Suit Murders*, and the non-fiction *Native Notes from the Land of Earthquake and Fire*. He has received fellowships from both the National Endowment for the Arts and the Guggenheim foundation.

This interview was conducted by Kay Bonetti, Director of the American Audio Prose Library. The Prose Library offers tapes of American authors reading and discussing their work. For information contact AAPL at P.O. Box 842, Columbia, MO 65205.

An Interview with Thomas Sanchez / *Kay Bonetti*

Interviewer: Mr. Sanchez, you've described your life as being somewhat Dickensian. Certainly your books deal with extremes—extremes of behavior, extremes of circumstance. Does your work reflect the extremes of your life?

Sanchez: It probably has, but I never thought that my life was extreme. You feel that the way you are living is the way everyone lives, especially when you're a child. My father died in World War II on an aircraft carrier that went down in the Pacific three months before I was born. My earliest memories are of having nightmares of being on fire and drowning.

Interviewer: And eventually your mother became so ill that you ended up in the St. Francis School for Boys. Can you tell us about that?

Sanchez: It was kind of a combination orphanage and boarding school and reform school. Most of the children there were either very poor children or orphans. There were Chicano children, there were American Indians, there were black children. It was a true American melting pot. It seems rather simplistic, but I really did live in a kind of "Family of Man" situation. A very tough one at times and a very dangerous one at times. But one which gave me a concept of what life could be outside the confines of that particular school.

Interviewer: Where was the school located?

Sanchez: It was in Watsonville, California, which is on the edge of the Monterey Bay in Northern California.

Interviewer: Is that near the Cannery Row of Steinbeck's novel?

Sanchez: Yes. Cannery Row is also on Monterey Bay. I spent some time living on the edge of Cannery Row when I was a kid, in particular as a teenager. When I was there, the Cannery Row that Steinbeck had written about, that ghostly presence, was still there. It had not yet been turned into chic boutiques and restaurants.

Interviewer: Did your mother work in the canning factories there?

Sanchez: No, but she did work in cannery factories on the east Bay of San Francisco, as did my grandmother.

Interviewer: To what do you attribute your early love of learning and literature, your attraction to writing?

Sanchez: It's difficult to find that moment of illumination, but, looking back, I think it goes to my grandmother. She was taken out of school at a very early age and for various reasons she didn't learn to read or write. She was ashamed of that, and I bring it up because it's important. She developed a sense of the oral; she developed a sense of storytelling. She could take the language, in particular the American language, and make something of it. She invented words and she had a real mastery of telling a story. She'd throw some verbs up in the air like they were a pizza pie and they would come down as a cherry pie. The postman and the neighbors would come along to have a cup of coffee in my grandmother's kitchen and stay for hours upon end.

She gave me a great gift without knowing it. She kept her very few precious objects in a little cedar box. Two of them were her favorite rosary and a very carefully folded and yellowing advertisement and review for my first novel, *Rabbit Boss*. When I discovered this after she died, I realized that for her the mystery

"The magic of words was equal with the spiritual world."

and the power that were held within that rosary also were held within the review of *Rabbit Boss*. The magic of words was equal to her with the spiritual world.

Interviewer: When I read *Rabbit Boss* my first outside reaction was, "How could anybody that young have written this book?" Do you feel like your childhood made you prematurely mature?

Sanchez: There's no question about that. A lot of *Rabbit Boss* goes back to when I was thirteen, fourteen years old in the boarding school with Native Americans. There really was an old Indian man who had some very young children. He was sort of a father to us all and in a spiritual way touched something in me and showed me a different consciousness. It was almost as if he was living in another dimension. I understood later what that dimension was and I tried to come to terms with it, and to explicate and explore it in *Rabbit Boss*. Although I do not write autobiographical novels, *Rabbit Boss* is obviously biographically informed as to its emotional thrust.

Interviewer: Your Family of Man experience at the St. Francis School seems to be reflected in your novels.

Sanchez: Right. The "Family of Man" that I was speaking of probably could more appropriately be referred to as the "Gang of Unruly Boys."

Interviewer: I'm assuming that your interest in Native American subject matter grew out of that experience.

Sanchez: More than an interest. This is where my living among Native Americans began, which extended to my adulthood—

"The continual sense of loss and the slate being wiped clean always set me apart."

working on ranches in the High Sierra with Washoe Indians and Indians of other tribes.

Interviewer: Was that before you went to San Francisco State?

Sanchez: Both before and during the time of. I was raised in a very curious way; when I was almost five my mother married a man who had a strongly identifiable WASP surname. I kept my surname because I was the last Sanchez of that line, but I grew up in an Anglo-Saxon world. Yet at the same time I was denied entrance into that world by the school system—if you had a Spanish surname you were pulled from class and taken off to be taught English as a second language. I had a sense that there was something different about me. If you didn't speak Spanish the kids who were primarily of Mexican descent wouldn't accept you as being a Latino. If you had a Spanish surname the children on the WASP side wouldn't accept you. This strange upbringing allowed me to be sort of the "other" and the "outsider."

Interviewer: So you did not speak Spanish as a small child?

Sanchez: No, no. My father was Spanish, but he was killed in the war. My mother was Portuguese and she did not speak Spanish. When my mother remarried, she married a man from the Midwest who certainly did not speak Spanish, but who did provide a particular kind of stable home life. The life did not remain stable because of outside forces. I was sent off to the boarding school/orphanage, and when I was a teenager our small farmhouse in rural California was condemned by the state to be part of a freeway system. The smashing of that farmhouse changed the course of my life yet again. That continual sense of loss and the slate being wiped clean always set me apart.

Interviewer: I read that when you were at the St. Francis school you were treated like you were—how did you say it, "destined for shop class." But a teacher there was taken by your verbal skills and your ability to write.

Sanchez: Yes. A history and English teacher recognized from my essays that I had a gift for language. When I left St. Francis, he called me in and said that God had given me a particular vocation and it would be a sin if I did not follow it. Now of course he felt that I would put that vocation into the hands of God and perhaps I would eventually be ordained in the priesthood. He had little notion that I would place that language in another service indeed.

Interviewer: How did you come to go to college? Did you go on scholarship?

Sanchez: No, I never had a scholarship in my life. I went to a community college in the Sacramento Valley. I'd always wanted to be a writer but had no concept of how it was done or how one made a connection with that life. When I was a young boy what came through about writers was that these were men who were in the world, who were acting on the world stage. They were going off and coming back with stories to tell—of another time, of another place. Obviously, this was long before I discovered the works of Elizabeth Bishop and Flannery O'Connor. In the community college there were, to my good fortune, two very young literature teachers who had come from Stanford. We discovered one another and I was almost tutored to what they had learned at Stanford—I got from them a sort of second-hand Stanford education. Then I went on to San Francisco State and studied in the Creative Writing department in the 1960s.

Interviewer: During the sixties you became extremely active in the anti-war movement. How did this relate to your writing life?

Sanchez: It was central to my life because I had lost a father in war. Also some of the boys that I grew up with in boarding school were among the first to die in Vietnam. Others were some of the first to leave America because of their conscious choice to no longer live in this country because of its actions in Vietnam. So I really could see a tremendous dichotomy within that extended family. I questioned the war because I understood the ramifications of war. For me it was not a distant, abstract thing.

Interviewer: When you became active in the anti-war movement were you already writing?

Sanchez: I was already writing, but the anti-war movement was part of something much larger. I was active in the Sacramento Valley in the 1960s when the earliest grape strikes were taking place, for example. I was also involved with CORE and SNCC, the Student Non-violent Coordinating Committee, before it became all black. I developed a particular kind of social consciousness which I had no notion at that particular time was enormously unfashionable. It almost hearkened back to the agrarian days of the likes of Frank Norris and even John Steinbeck.

Interviewer: Do you see a relationship between your life as an activist and your life as a writer?

"Our being in Vietnam was an extension of our westward thrust as a country."

Sanchez: I feel writing is an action which has ramifications. To tell you that I have no politics is probably the most political statement that anyone can make. But I think that the kind of politics we normally get involved in conspires against a writer and I have tried to stay one step ahead of that particular bullet.

Interviewer: People identified *Rabbit Boss* with the Vietnam novel. Was that your intent?

Sanchez: Absolutely. Our being in Vietnam was an extension of our westward thrust as a country—our completion of continental integrity. For me, the beginning of trying to deal with the war in Vietnam was to re-create the beginning of a war that took place on the western continent of the United States—the war against the indigenous peoples. It was an undeclared war, but it was a war nevertheless that almost destroyed the Native Americans. *Rabbit Boss* begins in 1846 with the Washoe Indians observing the cannibalization of the Donner party on the shores of Donner Lake in the High Sierra. It obviously was a moment when a particular kind of history began. There is also the great irony that the so-called civilized man is devouring himself on the shores of Donner Lake while the so-called *savage* who's witnessing this is quite well dressed, quite warm, and quite well fed.

That was their first encounter with the white man, and to this day, there are some Washoe that still believe the White Man is a cannibal. Indeed the Sierra Nevada was cannibalized, its natural resources were cannibalized; the Washoe, eventually, were almost obliterated from their original lands.

Even though *Rabbit Boss* ends in the 1950s, clearly before the Vietnam War begins, it stood in my mind as a metaphor that was infused by the war of Vietnam. I felt that I had to come to terms

"Working with the novel was like working with a tool of the enemy."

with America. The Chinese have a saying, "The gateway to the future is through the past." I really felt that *Rabbit Boss* was that link.

Interviewer: Yet you had to leave America—and the past—to write it. Why did you go away?

Sanchez: By 1969 we had landed on the moon and yet we were still waging this war in Vietnam. Every thirty minutes on the radio we're announcing body counts—how many of them we'd killed, how many of ours were killed. A rather cynical abstraction had taken place. No longer were we dealing with flesh and bone and blood and American youth—it was like some sort of cosmic sports event that was being toted up every day in the collective American mind. Shortly before I left America in 1969 there was a strike at San Francisco State University. It had become a very violent strike; a SWAT team was moving across the campus commons and clubbing students to the ground. There was a lot of blood and the students ran up the steps to the library and attempted to get in, but the library doors had been locked. The students who were trapped on the steps of the library were beaten and I remember quite vividly this image of the blood flowing down the steps and thinking what a profound irony: that inside all the learning is locked up and outside we are clubbing the youth of this country.

At that point I decided that the only way to survive would be to leave America to complete *Rabbit Boss*. It was also a time when the word, the novel, was very much looked down upon. If you wanted to make your statement, basically you grabbed a guitar, plugged it in, then sang your angst over the radio airwaves. Working with the novel was like working with a tool of the enemy; it was an

unfashionable thing to do. So I left in 1969 to write *Rabbit Boss*;
I went to the mountains in the south of Spain.

Interviewer: Why did you pick that particular story to tell, the
story of the Washoe?

Sanchez: I wanted to tell the story of a very seemingly insignificant
tribe of people, about which a letter to an Indian commissioner
stated, "there are fewer than 500 left; there's no reason to put any
lands aside for them because they're riddled with disease." Well, of
course we brought the disease—we brought venereal disease, we
brought alcoholism. And he said, "there's no reason to put land
aside because they'll all be dead soon enough." What an amazing
act of cultural arrogance. I wanted to reconstruct what that world
was, to show how much we lost as a country, as a people.

Interviewer: You went to Spain to write *Rabbit Boss* when the
first moon landing took place. I think it's a delicious irony that
several years later, unable to get a handle on another novel that
you wanted to write, you went to Key West, where you began
to hear the voices that turned into *Mile Zero* at the time of the
first space shuttle.

Sanchez: I never thought of that before. That's curious because
those were two very important moments of my life and also in
my fiction.

Interviewer: I see throughout your work the acute awareness that
the First World has been living at the expense of the Third World.
Mile Zero can be seen, I think, as the Third World's revenge on
the First World in the form of cocaine. All the elements are the

same: the collusion of the natives, the white man penetrating into the forest of the Third World people, and the Third World people acting in complicity.

Sanchez: That operates on many levels in *Mile Zero*. One of them I think you put your finger on very astutely: *Mile Zero* opens with the first space shuttle launch in America. One of the characters— the entity of Zobop—perceives this not as a great technological leap forward but as the firing of a virus into a pure universe.

At the same time a boatload of Haitian refugees is coming ashore, fleeing their own country because Baby Doc's regime had taken the poorest country in the Western Hemisphere and made it even poorer. They were willing to risk shark-infested seas, they were willing to risk dehydration or starvation. At the same time in Key West you could see this shift from a marijuana mentality to a cocaine reality. Cocaine was going to alter forever the spirit of America. If you were a smart kid on a fast boat in slow water under a full moon you could make yourself hundreds of thousands, if not millions, of dollars in a very short time. Here you have these three extraordinary situations coalescing at a particular geographical point in America which was the end of the road—Mile Zero, Key West, the eye of the last island as you go down the continental United States on the East Coast, where the road ends. It's the end of the road *or* it's the beginning of the American dream or the beginning of the final nightmare, depending on how you want to perceive it.

Interviewer: At the end of *Mile Zero*, St. Cloud walks out of the water and takes the hand of his friend, Justo, but we know that Justo may very well have contracted AIDS. Of course, the novel is full of all these deaths of Key West in the past; when the

"If you were a smart kid on a fast boat in slow water under a full moon you could make millions in a very short time."

cigar industry died something came along to replace it. What's now come along to replace everything at this point in the novel is cocaine. Can you talk a bit about that ending?

Sanchez: The fact that Justo may have AIDS, the fact that cocaine is also another form of a plague doesn't mean that it will be the end of the world. We've faced these plagues before. At the very end of the novel we're right at the cusp of the world changing again. It's in our capacity if we have an awareness of that particular fact to change the course of our own particular destiny. I believe in the power of the American novel—the power of the novel itself, the power of art itself, to persuade or dissuade, to make people aware, but not on an obvious level. Some of the last words spoken in the novel are that Christ is coming back, too. The Messiah, to me, is our ability to take action, to change the course of events, to make a world that we can abide in, that will not destroy us. That is not an easy task. And it is not a message that most people are willing to accept because it is a seditious message. It is saying, "If you don't change it, it is doomed."

Interviewer: How does "el Finito" fit into the scheme?

Sanchez: It can be taken on many different levels. There's the obvious one, of course: "el Finito," the absolute hurricane, the force of nature which will wipe the slate clean before mankind has a chance to destroy the slate. It also can be taken on the metaphoric level as that of nuclear holocaust.

Interviewer: That fits in with the structural imagery of the hoop of fire: the gulf stream is a circle, and of course a hurricane is a big circle. That informs the language through the entire novel.

"You begin a sentence in one place and it's almost like you're on an ice floe."

Sanchez: The language was one of the most difficult things to come to terms with. Having been in San Francisco I felt that the Vietnam generation had not been *portrayed* in American literature and American film so much as it had been *betrayed*. I wanted to get back to a particular essence of idealism that existed before the time of burnout. People don't realize that in order to be burned out you have to be on fire first. The moment that I really wanted to begin with was the moment of fire—that moment of commitment, that moment of extraordinary, overwhelming idealism of an entire generation. But I was on the lam from my own book, in a sense, and I headed out to the Caribbean to get a different venue, a different distance. I stopped, fortuitously, in Key West, and I realized I was in this emerging American metaphor and that I had to come to terms with it. I was in a very important geographical and political and emotional place at a moment in time. I seized upon that and I stayed in Key West.

Interviewer: And you started hearing voices.

Sanchez: The language for *Mile Zero* was mercurial. You begin a sentence in one place and it's almost like you're on an ice floe. By the time you get to the end of that sentence, you're somewhere else. There are moments on the flats outside of Key West when the water appears to be running uphill. I was trying to do this with the language, to move it in a way that it would have the ability to change course. It was an almost impossible task because it depended on the reader's trust. I had to prove to the reader in the opening passages of *Mile Zero*—all of book one—that we're going someplace, we're taking a journey, and we cannot know where that journey will lead us. What's important here is the journey itself. You can only develop that bond with the reader through the language in the early stages of the novel.

Interviewer: Where do you put yourself in the argument about the function of fiction in the twentieth century—that the writer creates an object that defies communication, that characters are no more than linguistic constructs, as opposed to the more traditional, realistic vision of fiction?

Sanchez: I think that the language is meaningless unless it's informed by emotion, that emotion is meaningless unless it's informed by an intellect. Each novel is a singular act of creation which creates and achieves or doesn't achieve its own goals and its own rules. It's almost impossible to compare one novel to another. I can't even compare my own novels one to the other—they're disparate and singular entities. The debate really couldn't interest me less because I fashion novels in a way that makes a particular kind of emotional and intellectual sense to me in terms of where I want to end up. I always know with the novel where it will end; I never know how I will get there.

Interviewer: Why did you take *Rabbit Boss* out of print?

Sanchez: I needed to get back to that time when I was an anonymous writer, I needed to get back to a place where I could create a whole language from a new imagination for me. I had become the man who wrote *Rabbit Boss* rather than Thomas Sanchez, the writer. I had not so much written myself out with *Rabbit Boss* as I had written myself in. Over that seven-year period I had obliterated in many ways my own ego. I had to come back to that place that allowed me to create a novel.

Interviewer: What do you mean when you say you had written yourself in?

Sanchez: When you move so deeply into a novel that its consciousness takes over your consciousness, it begins to supersede your own life. It devours you, it consumes you, it takes over your subconscious, it takes over your dream state. I would wake up in the middle of the night gnashing the insides of my cheeks with nightmares. I had placed a comma in the wrong place for the character who existed eighty years ago, and since that comma was in the wrong position in the sentence—that's not where that man would have stopped to take a breath—I had betrayed that character, which meant I had betrayed the chapter which meant I had betrayed the entire novel and all of those years were worthless. I would wake up with blood in my mouth and spit it out into a bowl. That kind of obsession with detail is a way that you write yourself in. It's writing yourself to a point where the ego that began the book no longer exists. That's a very dangerous place to be. You never know if you are going to come back from that particular journey.

Interviewer: And you felt like you hadn't?

Sanchez: I definitely had not. I have the feeling that it takes as long to un-write a novel as it takes to write one.

Interviewer: As I understand it, you made quite a bit of money on *Rabbit Boss* when it first came out. There was a big movie option, you bought a house in California, and then you took *Rabbit Boss* out of print.

Sanchez: Right. *Rabbit Boss* was optioned for $500 while I was

"What was important was that the shadow of Vietnam fall across the entire novel."

writing it; it then went up to a $1000 option. I had no idea if I was ever going to be paid for the novel. The first novel I wrote was rejected out of hand by many publishers. The second novel, *Rabbit Boss*, was turned down several times before it was finally optioned by Alfred Knopf. There were ten years where I had very little income. I worked at odd jobs as everything from a truck driver to a college teacher to a carpenter to a laborer to a gardener. When I sold the film rights to *Rabbit Boss* I was in a very curious position; I was not a good credit risk so I hadn't been able to run up a good deal of debt. I had hard cash during the bottom of the Nixon recession. I bought a house, which I eventually sold in order to write *Mile Zero*.

Interviewer: Where did the IRS come in?

Sanchez: The IRS certainly wanted to take its lion's share out of my earnings. That is true for most writers. The problem with working on a book for ten years or so is that you can't roll back in terms of taxes over that entire period of time. You're only allowed by law to go back so many years.

Interviewer: It must have taken an enormous act of will to work on *Mile Zero* as long as you did, given the volatile nature of its material.

Sanchez: Yes, I think probably the most difficult part was the MK character. In *Mile Zero*, MK originally existed in two books called MK's Book One and MK's Book Two. I realized about five years into *Mile Zero* that the material was pulling the novel too far back into the past of Vietnam. Key West gave me the bridge into the post-Vietnam realities of America. After being in Central America

"I think the cheapest play of all in this day and age is to write the horror of it all."

and writing book one of MK, I realized that the novel had to succeed as a novel of a future yet untold, a future yet undreamed. I had to remove MK. That was probably the most devastating moment for me. What really bothered me wasn't the fact that I was being shot at by both sides all over Central America. I had spent that much time on something that didn't last in the novel. After I completed the novel I realized that it was something that had to be written in order to inform what was left. What was important was that the shadow of Vietnam fall across the entire novel of *Mile Zero* and inform all of its actions.

Interviewer: The action of the novel is in 1981, yet many things that have happened since reverberate in that novel, among them the explosion of the space shuttle Challenger.

Sanchez: Well, that's ironic. Justo Tamarindo strolls out onto the scene at Mallory Dock and he is saying, *"Mal dia*, everything has gone bad today, what can happen next?" and he says, "The next thing that's going to happen is the space shuttle is going to fall out of the sky." That was written years before that event actually took place. Virtually a decade has gone by and the primary and dominant themes of *Mile Zero* are ironically still at the forefront of our American consciousness: cocaine, Central America. . . .

Interviewer: How do you feel about the novel that's left now? By taking MK out, an ambiguity about him runs like a thread through the entire novel.

Sanchez: Americans look at television and they see this shadow play in a box and they think that is reality. I wanted to create that same sense in a novel, that reality is out there someplace; I wanted that sense of uncertainty to prevail. The shadow of MK falls across the entire novel, very much as the events of Vietnam still fall across our daily lives.

Interviewer: Did you consciously allow the shadow of Joseph Conrad to fall across the figure of MK?

Sanchez: I did not. I did not want to write another "Up the River with Mr. Kurtz" book. I think the cheapest play of all in this day and age is to write the horror of it all. We know the horror of it all. I really wanted to begin the novel from that point of consciousness—not the journey up the river, but what happens when you're at the end of the river and you take your first step onto terra firma and it's not so firm. It's very soft; it's quicksand, and there are no rules; there is only a journey about to begin.

Interviewer: Did it occur to you that crafty critics might see the initials and think Mistah Kurtz?

Sanchez: That *never* occurred to me. I'm sure that crafty critics can think of all kinds of crafty things like that if they set their crafty little minds to it.

Interviewer: There are people who call this book a crime novel, a Gothic mystery novel.

Sanchez: I know. It's as if I've written twelve different books. Every single review focuses on a different character, a different element, a different slant—a mystery novel, a love story, a novel of the occult, a holy terror of a book. It goes on and on and on: some will say that the center of the novel is Justo Tamarindo, the

Cuban-African cop; some will say the center of the novel is St. Cloud, the burned-out political activist; some people will say it's MK. Some people say that the novel is about Key West; some people say the novel is about America today. It's all of those things and to isolate one element is to do a disservice to the novel. I see it as a metaphysical drama. That concept folds into the overview of what the novel sets for itself in the beginning to accomplish and resolve.

Interviewer: How did you structure the plot?

Sanchez: When I began the novel I knew that there was a sense of something beyond evil loose in the streets. I wasn't certain what form it was going to take. The AIDS virus was little known to the American public at the time. I was working on a novel where there was a virus that no one had a name for, no one knew what form it took, no one knew how it was being passed. I had no idea that the ramifications would be so enormous. I realized that it was imperative to retain the fact that the real sense of evil that we confront is the evil that we do one to the other, mankind, and what we're doing to the most endangered species, which is the planet itself. That is really what *Mile Zero* gets at. So that element of suspense and surprise that comes climactically in *Mile Zero* is not really how the novel is resolved. The novel is resolved on another level.

Interviewer: Do you see one of the functions of your work as trying to restore the knowledge of all of America, the other America, the America that isn't taught in the history classes?

Sanchez: I don't really see a novelist in the role of a teacher.

"What happens at the end of the river when you take your first step onto terra firma and it's not so firm? It's quicksand, there are no rules, only a journey about to begin."

Perhaps not even as a seeker. I think that if you actually can give life to a book, that *perhaps* that life will touch other lives in a meaningful way, but only *perhaps*. Writing a novel is a fabulous act of arrogance. If I'm going to place a novel before someone and it takes them five or seven hours or twenty hours to read, I want to make certain that I'm placing before them the very best that I'm capable of, something that I've thought out in every single word, with every single line. It must have a purpose and a value. Otherwise, I would not offer it.

EGGPLANTS / *David Wojahn*

—After Amy Wilentz

You must understand: we have done the Lord's work here
   since 1961. Eldon had just
      finished the seminary, and I was only twenty,
though I suppose you're thinking you could never
   picture me as a girl, and sometimes I think

I never was. You see the snapshot there:
   Eldon and I on the airport runway, coming in
      to Port-au-Prince, my absurd gray woolen suit
and pillbox hat! Even Baptists wanted
   to look like Mrs. Kennedy. And the heat

that day—like a hammer. I'll never forget
   how I prayed just for the strength to walk
      the tarmac into Customs. Then a night in a filthy
hotel, and next day our ride up the Route Nationale—
   just a gully, like a riverbed—to here.

You journalists: I've seen your sort every year
   since Duvalier took power. You'll sip
      from your lemonade, so prim in that dress,
so polite. But away from here you're a slut,
   and everything I say to your little machine

will come out in print as lies, as ridicule.
   "Mrs. Cunningham believes in prayer... "
      You'll see the hymns the congregation sings—
Amazing Grace in their own Creole—
   as some fancy ironic symbol. You'll call us

fundamentalists, imperialists,
   as if you weren't one too.
      But the hymns, you must admit how beautiful
they sound, though I don't know my Creole
   very well. You see, we try to teach them English:

so many families leave the countryside
   for Port-au-Prince, the shantytowns, and they're
     better off with some English. They can find
good work in the hotels. Be honest with me—
   admit they're little more than beasts, that God

has His work cut out for Him. And even God
   would tell you so. Have you seen how they live?
     continually in fear and superstition.
That scarecrow in the garden with the crushed
   derby hat, the tattered black frock coat, that's Baron

Samedi, the lord of the Dead. The derby,
   it's his symbol. And Duvalier would dress
     that way, to make them think the Baron was
on terms with him. The Baron sipping rum
   in the Presidential Palace! It was said

an elevator ran from hell straight up
   to Papa Doc's bank vault. And they all *believe*
     such drivel! Clarvius, our gardener,
for two years he was convinced he was a zombie,
   held slave to some village sorcerer, though you won't

get him to talk of it. And dogs gone wild
   that howl from the hills past sundown: they say
     they're *loups garous*, werewolves who live off babies'
blood. Oh, they file into church on Sundays,
   but they're here for the meal we feed them later,

though they'd rather eat their horrid cassava
   than the soup and beans the Mission freights
     from Dallas. Lord Jesus is as far from them
as we are from a shopping mall, though Eldon
   says it's sin to talk this way. Here's a story

for your article: there was this woman
   in the church, a clean decent woman who kept
     to herself. I knew her, not too well, but on
Sundays I would say hello, chat awhile
   about the market, the weather. The woman

raised eggplants in her field, very plump
and firm. Market days, she'd get up early—
two in the morning—and wake her daughter
who'd pick the eggplants while the mother held
a candle, and they'd cart them in the dark

to the market at Passe Reine, arrive before
sunrise, set up their stall, the eggplants huge,
so purple they seemed black. By daybreak,
when the neighbors arrived with their own eggplants,
the two had already sold what they had brought

and were heading home. So the neighbors had a rough
time selling eggplants: the pair had a monopoly
on the Passe Reine eggplant market, just because
they'd get up before their shiftless neighbors!
So the neighbors began to talk. The women

were this, the women were that. The mother clearly
was a sorceress: she'd call on evil
spirits to wake her in the night, when no one
else would think of rising. She fed the demons on
the livers of children. You see, a girl

had died in sleep a couple fields away.
And the daughter? She had hair on her arms
and a clubfoot—easy to conclude she was
a *loup garou*. but as I say, the pair
just kept to themselves, continued to take

their early morning walks. But then last May,
when the sun was still down, a mob of neighbors
confronted them—the two of them were just
coming out the door, the eggplant baskets
balanced on their heads. At first the crowd

just insulted them, but the pair was silent,
kept on walking. Maybe that's what provoked
the neighbors so, for they started to beat
the woman with sticks, and when the daughter tried
to hold them back, they beat her too, and finally—

you know what's coming, don't you?—they stoned them to death.
    By afternoon it got back to the Mission,
        and Clarvius brought me down the road to see
for myself, the crowd still milling around.
    It was then I saw her and I just... Well,

her face, it wasn't *there* anymore. There was
    no face. Hamburger, that's what it was like....
        And the daughter, they shoved a stick up her....
You think I *like* to talk about it?.... And
    the crowd by now, it was fifty or sixty

and who knows how many were involved, not just
    the neighbors, but dozens of them, hundreds,
        everyone I'd see in church on Sundays.
Our cleaning girl, Celeste, she told me how the crowd,
    when the bodies stopped moving, picked up

the baskets, divided the eggplants up, and sold them,
    those very eggplants, at the market that day.
        Imagine—they must have still had blood
trickling down their hands. And Celeste, she was
    laughing when she told me. I know: you'll say

it's part of faith, that I should try to forgive
    such things, understand these people
        and their savagery. But first they must
repent. Even you must know the scripture:
    Repent, saith the Lord. Unrepentant,

they are unrepentant. Tolerance?
    Don't talk to me of tolerance. The other day
        this young girl, black as coal, she comes up to me,
and stares at me in that wide-eyed way,
    white cotton church dress, and she says *Madame....*

I bend down to her. She reaches up and takes
    my hair—you know the way they do? Because
        they like to touch white women's hair. And she
holds it carefully, as though she's studying it.
    Then she drops it, and she says to me, right in

my face, *loup garou, loup garou, loup garou.*

A MAP / *David Wojahn*

i.

Tomb Figures: Stonecutters' Cemetery, Barre, Vermont

She bears her swooning husband up in stone,
And lets him ease his hammer down, his livelihood
A psilocosis sediment—plundered lungs
That killed him at fifty, an end he hurried

Each evening and Sunday of those years he chiselled
At the granite block in his garage. Larger,
Of course, than life, they loom and sprawl, detailed
Indifferently, faces square as Toltec warriors'.

So what survives of them is love, not art,
Some eloquence of gesture wholly unseen
In her botched and massive apron folds, the .part
In his hair, surreally precise. Acid rain
Will scour even this away: twenty years
Returns them to faceless rock. Their dates already blur.

ii.

Five Thousand Terra Cotta Warriors

Like barbers with scissors, the workmen clear
The dirt away, brushing from the necks down.
As in childbirth, the heads are first to appear,
But mustached scornful, jutting up from chain-

Mail, leather collars. Spawn of dragon's teeth, they've slept
Two thousand years, guardians of His Majesty Ch-in Shih
Who built the Great Wall and wondrous cities, kept
Eight hundred concubines, two million warriors, and decreed

That all scholars, poets, and Taoist priests
Be buried alive. When the Son of Heaven Himself

Expired, on a journey to Canton, His scheming eunuchs
Sought to keep it secret, propped Him on a litter, a scarf

Against His face, and bore Him through crowds to the palace
    gates
With a cart of salted fish to mask His stench.

iii.

Valley of the Fallen, Castile, 1987

Convict labor, eight million dead, and a colonel's
Morbid hubris drilled a hole inside
This mountain, under a cross ten stories tall.
Dark basilica, where paramilitary monks stand guard

Around the stone where Franco smugly sleeps,
Bordered by kitsch, the bogus modern tapestries
And stained glass meant to echo zealot Philip's
Inquisitional Golden Age. VIVA LA MUERTE's

Graffiti-ed above a restroom urinal
By FRANCO FUE EL HIJO DE PUTA,
The war still waged in number two pencils,
The verb *morir* the country's reigning motto.

Farmers still churn up mass graves beneath their ploughs.
Firing squad: the eight commands six deadly zeroes.

iv.

Neanderthal Burial, The Field Museum

Traces of red ochre, a necklace of the canine
Teeth of giant elk, a flint knifeblade
And fossil pollen residue display an afterlife
Greeted both with spears and poppy garlands.

This broken-skulled hunter, crippled by arthritis,
Venerable at forty, shall rise again to endless herds
Of mastodon, though a caption tells us

His half-formed larynx was not capable of words,

And thus his thinking never turned abstract
Enough to foresee doom, or its aftermath—
Five mourners at a forest clearing plot, silent
While soil and blossoms spatter the chinless face.

So the after life is wordless, concrete as death
Itself. The mourners stumble mutely up the path.

v.

Fort Snelling National Cemetery, St. Paul, 1990

Mutely up the path, into drizzle and mud,
We climb the squat hill to the freshest graves
And scan three miles of headstones, unadorned,
Identical—war dead, veterans, and their wives.

A Northwest DC Seven lumbers up
Unmutely overhead: at night this place is seared
By runway lights. How do the fallen sleep?
Memorial Day weekend, and the earth has sprouted

Innumerable plastic lilies. We've followed a map
To find this plot, marked with a felt pen X.
And at last, head bent, cap off, my father weeps.
I have to stop here now. The bucket of ash

Beneath the stone. Runway lights flaring on in rain,
Jet fuel smell, the whine. And this is my mother's grave.

LATE EMPIRE / *David Wojahn*

—17 & 1988

The hours, ripe apples, hang. The pleasure boats
  dapple the artificial lake, the women
    shadowed by silk parasols, hands caressing water,

the men in powdered wigs, half-dozing at
  the oars, and above the palace of Versailles
    the *globe airostatique*, tasselled and swollen,

a Faberge egg, labors to the sky
  with its wicker basket cargo—a puzzled drake,
    a rooster, a goat dubbed *Climb-into-Heaven*—

the brays and crowing wavering above
  a hundred thousand pointing fingers, and the din
    giving way to collective gasp, the one breath

inhaled, exhaled, novitiates all; the halcyon
  days before the bells or sirens peel, blackout,
    a night sky bristling with searchlights. But here?

The Screaming Blue Messiahs erupt from the stage.
  Drums hiss at bass; the giant shaved-headed
    singer strikes a pose, a chord, hulking

maniacally into *The Wild Blue Yonder*
  amid a light show of divebombers—Stukas—careening
    ever downward, feedback ricocheting

the walls. London, the Town and Country Club,
  and I've lost you in a riot of green spiked hair,
    slam dance, combat boots, the crowd awaiting

the next upheaval, the storming of the palaces
  of the *ancien régime....If I die in a combat zone*
    box me up and ship me home. Footage

of fire, Dresden and its million pounds of napalm,
   the singer clubbing his guitar to wire
      and splinters on the stage, and I've lost you

to the noise and tidal dancefloor. *I am*
   the destroyer, I am the des-troy-er.
      A skinhead waves a broken bottle at

a scared Bengali kid, and the light show
   bends their fight to slow-mo; the kid leans down,
      hugs himself while his friends crowd by, his sleeve

in bloody shreds. The room speaks the language
   of last summer's recurring dream: the terrible
      incinerating light has come, the dead

frozen black to the wheels of their cars, and I weave
   a path among them to a house no longer standing,
      call you in the way I call you now,

deaf to my own voice, and it's now
   I see you lifted skyward by the crowd,
      passed with half a dozen others on raised arms,

weightlessly buoyed to the music's stammer,
   passed forward and backward across the dancefloor,
      a zig-zag slither, until you finally come to rest,

earthbound again, on wobbly feet by a dull red
   EXIT sign, and I'm threading my way through the faces
      to reach you, shards of the guitar tossed snarling

to a sea of hands.... And when the balloon reaches
   three hundred feet, an early fall wind propels it
      beyond the lake, His Majesty's deer park,

the ersatz peasant village of the Queen,
   and when it blunders and falls to a field ten miles
      away, imagine the terror-struck farmers and milkmaids

lamenting the fall of the moon. Before them the goat,
   no longer dazed, grazes on some clover;
      the broken-winged rooster staggers in circles.

Now fear has raised a hundred pitchforks and scythes.
   Now the fallen moon, and its cargo, must die.
      How can we blame them? They set the field on fire.

LILLY, MY SWEET / *Judy Ruiz*

T HERE'S SOME THINGS I want you to know. When that
woman set herself on fire, she had a reason. When I watched
her burn, I had a reason. This is no trial. I already went through
enough of that, not that it was a real trial. It was a bunch of
doctors and some nurses and me, and we sat around a big oak
table and I screamed twice.

I screamed when Dr. Cavasulu asked me, "Why you not help
her not burn?" And I had reasons for screaming. My reasons get
mixed up in my head now, just like they did when he asked the
question. I go back to that day and how I smoked my cigarette
and watched the leaves swirl on the lawn, and I could see the
woman's skirt on fire and how the flames looked like the leaves.
Pretty soon the flames were outside the window, swirling, and
the woman danced in a skirt of autumn.

The second time I screamed was when another doctor said,
"Well, I think this whole matter tells us that Lilly is where she
needs to be." Lilly is me. Where I need to be is on the moon,
not in a conference room in a state institution that I have named
Bewildered Palms. I need to be on the moon with some oxygen
and a good book.

I call the place Bewildered Palms in honor of Margaret and
Joan. Margaret's the skinny one who will stand for hours with
one hand up in the air and her other hand covering her mouth.
Then a nurse will come along and take Margaret's hand down out
of the air and take the other hand away from her mouth while
Margaret's blue eyes focus on the linoleum. The nurse will take
her to a chair and sit her down and say, "There. That's better."
Margaret will stare at the floor for a while, but pretty soon she'll
start looking at her hands, turning them so she can see her palms,
then so she can see the backs, then palms up again. Next, she'll
say, "No. Oh, no," bolt upright out of the chair, assume her
hand-in-the-air, hand-to-mouth position, as if she has just read
her own fortune of terror.

Joan is fat and walks like a toddler. At medicine time, she holds
her thorazine pills in her left hand until the orange color starts
to come off. The nurse will say, "Joan, put your pills in your
mouth now," and Joan will grin, squeeze her left hand into a fist,

and start her little dance from one foot to the other, a swaying she has to do. And she has to do it until she's done. I saw her get those pills four times a day every day for as long as I was there, and every time the nurse would say the same thing and Joan would sway. On and on. The dance of bricks. If I'd have been the nurse, I'd have mashed those pills up and stuck them in her biscuits about day two.

When Joan got finished dancing, she'd swallow her pills and open her hand, holding it up for the world to witness the orange smudges on her palm. Then she'd pat her palm to first the right and then the left cheek, rouging herself up for the finale: she'd lick her palm and wipe it on her dress. Miracle accomplished while the rest of us waited in line.

My own palms held no surprises. Both of them square as a hoe blade, and a small scar in the center of the right one from when I'd stuck a hairpin into an electrical outlet when I was two, a jolt that blew me halfway across the living room, so my mother says.

I just thought of this: maybe you don't trust me now that you know where I was. Well, I'm not there anymore. Not that it makes any difference in my thinking, which only slowed down a few hours a week anyhow, and then only after some goons held me down while some other goon threw a switch that made my head light up in a blue arc. I'd come to in a daze of dumbness. The dumbness would last at most a day, and then I'd be right back to my old self, throwing my panties out the window.

You might appreciate this: during one doctor/me meeting, I was asked just exactly what did I want to do with my life. It's one of those doctor-questions that folks like me always get wrong while thinking we got it right. So I said, "Well, I'd like to live sweet-breathed and naked." I always answered those questions as honestly as I knew how, thinking I was sane, thinking I'd get out. And always I'd end up over in occupational therapy gluing elbow macaroni on to a cigar box or lacing up a wallet through those pre-punched holes or painting the inside of some ceramic bunny ears a nice shade of pink.

So maybe you're saying, "Sure. We've heard this story before. You want us to believe that you were sane and being kept in some back ward by mistake." It was no mistake. See, I was so crazy I thought one of my legs was bigger than the other one.

Now a thought like that might be OK if you kept it to yourself, but I couldn't do that *then*. I wasn't smart enough to know how to keep quiet. And this leg thing would come and go. One day

I'd be fine, and the next day my left leg would be twice the size of my right leg. Or more than twice. And I could see it even in a mirror. So when it first started happening, I'd tell people, and they'd look at my legs and say, "No. They're both the same size." Then I'd drag people with me over to a mirror and I'd say, "Look. Just *look.*" And they'd look and say, "No. They're both the same size." This always amazed me, this mirror part. I mean, I could understand how a person might not see what is really there when just looking at the really there thing, but a mirror, for God's sake, is proof.

So my father finally had had enough of all this leg stuff and he and my mother, one brisk day, shuffle me off to see a shrink. Well, it just so happened that both my legs were the same size when I went in to Dr. Dondee's office, but just when he's asking me what "A rolling stone gathers no moss" means, I feel my leg start to get big. I feel all this relief, you know, that it's happening at the doctor's office so that he can see it. I just *know* he will be able to see it. So I say, "Doctor, 'A rolling stone gathers no moss' means—look here at my leg—it's getting big right now—'A rolling stone gathers no moss' means don't ride your bicycle with roller skates on." I can hardly contain my happiness. Not only is my leg growing right here in his office, but I have also told him the meaning of a rolling stone gathering no moss.

Well, what I wish I had etched in stone is the exact look that came over his face while he looked at my father while my father looked at my mother. What Dr. Dondee had on his face was a grin, a grin I would grow to understand the full meaning of in my future dealings with doctor types, a grin that could only mean I had fallen neatly into some box labeled "Hallucinations. Rush Order." At first, I thought his grin meant that he could see my leg, which was getting bigger and bigger, so big, in fact, that I feared it might actually explode. Then my mother started her double-clutch crying and my father patted her back saying it all would be alright.

Then I burped, and a menthol smell came out of me, and my father smelled it and said, "There. There's that smell she has. She smells like Vicks Vapor Rub." He says to the doctor, "Come over here. Smell her."

Dr. Dondee said, "I can smell her from here."

"*Do something,*" my mother said. My mother had a way of getting paralyzed when anything other than cream of wheat was going on. I mean, she'd freeze up and say, "Do something." And it worked. People did things. Maybe it was the desperation in her voice, the pitifulness. When she said it, you could sort of imagine her going out of her chair backwards and careening around the room in a death wheeze if you didn't *do something*.

Once, we were out in the garage together. I was hitting rocks with a hammer. My father was organizing jars of nails. She came into the garage from the kitchen with a martini for my father. He always let me eat the olives. She put the drink down on his wooden work bench, said something about sawdust, and kissed him. She turned to go back into the kitchen, and that's when she saw the tarantula.

She put one hand to her throat and whispered very loudly, "Do something," and with her other hand she waved in the direction of the tarantula. Then she froze. My father grabbed the hammer out of my hand and hit at the tarantula, and the tarantula jumped what seemed like six feet straight up into the air, landing in a different place on the concrete floor. My father repeated the hit motion, the tarantula repeated the jump thing. I sat on the floor with my rocks and watched this hitting jumping thing go on for it seemed like ever. Finally, my father ripped his own shirt off and threw it over the tarantula and the show was over.

"You girls go in the house," he said. I knew he meant to kill what was small under his shirt on the garage floor. He scooped up the shirt and made a twist in it, like you'd do if you were going to crush some ice cubes in a towel, and just as my mother and I got into the house, there was the smallest sound of something hitting against something, and another and another. When he came into the kitchen, he dropped his shirt into the trash basket and said, "It's an old shirt."

"I can wash it," my mother said.

"No need," he said; but I still heard the smallest sound.

About a year later, I saw my father rip another shirt off. I was sleeping on a mattress on the floor and my mother came walking through the room backwards, the light from the living room pouring into my sleep, my father walking toward my backwards-walking mother. She had something in her hand and her hand was raised up and my father said, "Go ahead, Ruth. Go ahead. Kill me." He ripped his shirt open and the buttons popped off. One button rolled on its edge all the way over to the mattress where I sat blinking in my pajamas, and the light shined off of what my mother held poised at my father's chest.

The next thing I knew I was sitting on the toilet crying while my father told me that he and my mother were just acting out a play they had seen. Years later, I could close my eyes and see that button roll to me, and I would shudder at what my mother could have done, at what my father dared her to do. But this isn't the weird part. I thought my mother had a knife in her hand that night. I thought that for years. I asked her about it, finally. She laughed and said, "Oh, no, Lilly. It was a fork." Somehow, I was safer in my bed when I thought it was a knife.

I don't know how old I was when I found Valo. You've got to be an old addict to remember Valo. Little inhalers you could stick up your nose and sniff for a cold, only we'd bust the plastic containers open and eat the wicks inside them. Not the whole wick. One Valo inhaler could last eight hits. Cut the wick up and try to get it swallowed before the taste could get on your tongue. The best speed I ever did. Only there were side effects, like thinking one of your legs was bigger than the other. And burping eucalyptus vapors into the room. And the overwhelming need to polish chrome and clean ovens comes and paste wax the floors and wash the walls and arrange everybody's socks, then the flat, dead come down when the only thing you could know is a bunch of words being said in another life you could get to if you just had a gun to aim at your own head, one spark of energy left to pull the trigger; but what's this in my pocket? When did I shave my head? And just when did I shave the dog? It's the flat, dead comedown that caused the real trouble, caused folks like me to end up out at Bewildered Palms getting hooked up to the shock machines.

But I have to tell you about a rolling stone. I was nine and riding my bicycle with my roller skates on when I fell. I hit hard, right on my tail bone. So I dragged my bike home, had to crawl. When I got there, I hollered for help, hollered that I was hurt bad. My father heard me and came to stand at the top of the porch stairs. He had a twenty dollar bill in his hand and he said I could have it if I could walk up those stairs. Twenty dollars was a lot of money in 1951. A lot of money. Only my back was broken and I could not walk to get the money. Finally my father had to carry me into the house. He put me on the sofa, and I told him and my mother what had happened. My mother cupped my chin in her hand and looked into my eyes and said, "Lilly, my sweet. A rolling stone, you know, gathers no moss." I woke up in the hospital.

And then, years later, I woke up in the hospital again thinking one leg was bigger than the other. My roommate, Marilyn, was my age and her left hand was useless from when she had tried to cut if off. She tried to cut it off so she could bleed to death after she had drowned her baby in a bathtub. She never said a word to anybody, but the nurses told the rest of us, those of us with any sense left, what she'd done. They told us because they needed help in watching her. Suicide Watch they called it.

Some nights I'd lie awake and listen to her breathe. That's the only sound I ever heard her make, that even breathing. She never snored. One night I pretended she was my mother, and that I was the baby she had drowned. It scared me at first to think like that, but then this soft thing happened to me. It was just like getting born, only in reverse. For just a moment, I was loved.

One day when we were in our room, she set her skirt on fire. With my matches that I'd gone to a lot of trouble to get. I was mad and thought damn it, Marilyn—you would pull this shit when it's my turn to watch you. So there she is, standing with her skirt on fire, and then she looks right into my eyes. *I knew.* So I watched her and I smoked my cigarette and looked out the window and thought about how I didn't know God and about how I'd never done a decent thing in my life. It was just the burning woman and me, and I knew for just a tiny time all about grief and love, all I thought I'd ever need to know in this world. I let her burn until she died.

Judy Ruiz has a book of poems, *Talking Razzmatazz*, just published by University of Missouri Press. One of her essays appeared in *Best American Essays* in 1989.

The
Diary
of
Jean L. Clemens
New York
1900

To my dear Cousin
Ida, in remembrance of what I
hope is a rebegun friendship
never again to be broken —
Sept 26th 1911   from her very affectionate
Jean L. Clemens

DIARY OF JEAN L. CLEMENS—NEW YORK,
October 1900 / *Jean L. Clemens*

Picture the world as Jean Clemens must have seen it in 1900. A young woman who has grown up during ten years of travelling around Europe—the daughter of a man who is becoming not just a celebrity but something more like a supercelebrity, the toast of New York—yet she is haunted by uncertainties and fears, afraid of becoming an old maid because she is ill with a mysterious and somehow shameful disease—epilepsy. She has a knack for certain things—languages, carving—but she doesn't feel truly accomplished at anything. She loves music and the theater. She admires but is envious of her older sister Clara, whom she considers much more accomplished and romantically attractive than she is. Sister Clara can sing quite well, in fact is preparing for her debut as a mezzo-soprano. In some ways Jean lives her own romantic fantasies through her sister, at the same time competing with her.

Jean's childhood was spent in a fairy castle in Hartford, and she has fond but somehow painful memories of that place. She remembers the dark time when her father was becoming more and more distracted and finally ran out of money, fell into bankruptcy, and the family escaped to Europe. Yet somehow, through a magic that she doesn't fully understand, her father has become prosperous again. He remains the same lovable old rascal to Jean, but he seems unusually happy lately, seems almost to have become younger. He actually *looks* younger. Newspaper men are always coming by to find out what "Mark Twain" thinks about this or that. Famous actors and actresses send free tickets to plays. Her father's old friend, William Dean Howells, remains his friend, but acts vaguely puzzled by his increasing celebrity (Mr. Howells, however, is not nearly as interesting to Jean as his son, John Howells, one of the many young men courting her sister Clara).

While the Clemenses are not rich, still they are rubbing shoulders with some of the most prominent people in New York. Henry Rogers himself, the great organizer of Standard Oil, helps her father with some of his business transactions. And well her dear father can use such help, for he is an entrepreneur, a speculator, in his very bones—too often to his detriment.

Everyone in the family still suffers a deep sadness over the death of her sister Susy five years ago, from spinal meningitus. The family has had its share of illness. During Jean's infancy and childhood, someone in the family was always sick. When she was twelve years old, her mother became ill with acute hyperthyroid disease. At the same time, Jean herself began to suffer her strange mental spells and the sick, vaguely desperate feeling of not knowing who she was or what she was doing. . . . Her father at first thought she was merely acting willful and spoiled. For four turbulent years, in fact, he was really against her—until soon after Susy's death, when she was diagnosed as having epilepsy.

By 1900 Sam Clemens has become a thoroughgoing health faddist, involving himself in such things as "Plasmon," a colorless, tasteless food supplement that he claims "digests as easily as water" and yields the nutritional equivalent of "sixteen pounds of the best beef." He believes in it so much, in fact, that not only does he go around telling everybody to drink it, he also has invested a great deal of money in it. More importantly for Jean, he has become a believer in osteopathy, and a promoter and publicist for it. He has Jean taking sometimes very painful treatments for her epilepsy from osteopaths in England and Sweden, and now in New York from one Dr. Helmer, at 31st Street and Madison.

Why does Jean Clemens write a diary? Perhaps it is the one time when she feels that she can be fairly unguarded. She uses a common pencil, writing freely, seldom striking out a word. Insofar as the ingrained decorum of the late Victorian age allows her to, she can open up her heart. She doesn't worry about being interesting or clever, nor about whether she is being generous or not so generous; she just writes what has happened during the day, what she thinks about things, the daily concerns of life. She can't help but write about her illness; can't help but be concerned about the moments of confusion and forgetfulness that invade her mind. But it is, after all, her diary. Writing in it is like looking in a mirror and talking, almost absent-mindedly, to her own image. Perhaps it helps organize her life, helps make the pressures more bearable, and gives her a chance to savor the little triumphs.

For readers ninety years later, the diary is interesting as the record of a young American woman at the turn of the century, as she and her family try to establish a home in New York. It shows something of the stresses and strains of the late Victorian era—the guilts and pressures, the presence of death. Yet finally, Jean's diary is an interesting comment on the Clemenses, characterized by so many Twain biographers as a sad menagerie. It shows that for all their human weaknesses, they relied on and often enjoyed each other's company.

A Note on the Text

These selections come from the first of seven volumes of Jean Clemens' diary. A few changes have been made in spelling and punctuation. Volumes 2 through 7 were written during 1905–1907 in Dublin, N.H., and Ketonah, N.Y., concluding two years before Jean Clemens' death by drowning in a bathtub, due to a seizure.

According to Alan Jutzi, Curator of Rare Books at the Huntington Library, where all volumes reside, Jean's diaries were in the original inventory of items in Twain's estate made soon after his death; however,

Clara Clemens retained them along with certain other items (e.g., dedicated copies of *The Prince and the Pauper*) when the Twain papers were sold to the Huntington in the 1940s. At her death, Clara bequeathed the diaries to her personal secretary, whose executor sold the items to the Huntington six years ago.

Thanks to Robert Hirst, General Editor, Mark Twain Project, to Alan Jutzi of the Huntington, and to the other helpful people at that library.

Speer Morgan
Paul Zaul
Jo Sapp

Very well. Beautiful, warm day.

At the breakfast table I got what was both a great shock and a great surprise. Mamma had three telegrams inviting her to spend the night tomorrow night with three different people, one of them being Mrs. Warner[1] who had intended coming here to see us. I didn't suppose that Mamma so much as dreamed of going to Hartford, so was very much surprised to hear her talk about using me as an excuse for not spending the night.

I didn't say anything for some time and then said: "I only wish I had the chance." Mamma looked rather disgusted and said: "You have heard the news, haven't you?" I had heard nothing and said so. "Cousin Charlie[2] is dead," said she. I was simply taken off my feet, because although I thought he looked very old and not at all strong four years ago when I saw him, still it never occurred to me that there was any danger of his dying.

When we got upstairs Mamma told me the details. A farewell dinner had been given to Uncle Joe[3] before his European trip, and when the dinner was over (it had been given somewhere downtown), Cousin Charlie, who seemed as well as usual, said he was going to have his hair cut and would then walk home.

I believe he hadn't reached the barber's, when he began to feel a little dizzy. He was just going by a house which he knew about. I believe they had been very kind to some colored people in there, so he rang the bell, told the woman who opened the door that he felt dizzy and asked to be allowed to sit down.

The woman put him down on a sofa, made him comfortable, and then went out. She stayed away about ten minutes, and when she came back he was dead.

All this happened on **Saturday, October 20th, 1900.**

I shall be the only member of the family not at the funeral, they don't want me to go, so that they can use me as an excuse for not spending the night in Hartford.

---

[1] Susan Lee Warner, wife of Charles Dudley Warner, editor of *Hartford Courant* and collaborator on *The Gilded Age*. They had been MT's next-door neighbors.

[2] Charles Dudley Warner had just died in Hartford, at age 71.

[3] As with "Cousin Charlie," Joseph Hopkins Twichell was no relative but a dear family friend. He was the family clergyman in Hartford and MT's dearest friend there. The lunch (not dinner) Jean mentions was to celebrate his trip to Europe scheduled for 22nd October.

Everyone says that since Charlie had the grippe, and a little later pneumonia with paralysis of the face, that he had seemed very feeble and that he seemed to be sinking daily. If such is the case then it is of course a blessing that he died of heart failure and not of some long drawn out disease.

Are Susy[4] and he together now? And are they conscious of the people and the doings of this world? Or have they passed way above all pertaining to this sad life of ours? Why can't we know for sure what their thoughts and feelings are and whether Susy loves us, sees how we love and miss her? Oh Susy, do show yourself in some sure, certain way to some one of us! Do you forgive me my brutalities? Do let me know in some way, dear Susy.

It must have been this horrid illness that made me not realize your death and seem not to have any feelings at all, because now I very often feel the vacancy in our lives. I don't suppose I shall ever feel it the way Clara[5] did, because we were never such companions as you two or as we would be now.

I went again to Dr. Helmer and had my treatment,[6] which was rather painful again. I just lost myself before lunch, and then, after having my head washed, I slept an hour.

After dinner we really decided that Mamma had better not go to Hartford, because not only the physical but the emotional and mental strain would be so great.

Mamma likes a house in Washington Square, which she saw this morning with Mrs. Doubleday,[7] very much indeed, and the only thing which prevents our taking it at once is the price. We don't know as yet what the rental of it is. If we can't take this house, we shall probably take one of Mr. Walker's in Irvington, Papa is so set about getting out of New York's clutches. If we can come in conveniently then people can come as easily out to him. I do not want to go outside of New York, because although the country is perfectly beautiful, still I wanted to do a lot of work

[4] Eldest of the three Clemens girls, Olivia Susan, born 1872, had died of spinal meningitis in 1896, just as she and Jean were about to join the rest of the family in Europe.

[5] The middle sister, born 1874, she would wed the pianist Ossip Gabrilowitsch at age 35 and, widowed, would wed at 70 Jacques Samossoud, whose gambling debts wiped out her fortune—even to selling her father's library and papers. She died in 1962.

[6] George N. Helmer continued the osteopathic treatments begun in England and Sweden by Dr. Heinrick Kellgren's clinic—a triweekly series of treatments.

[7] Her husband Frank assumed the presidency of Doubleday–Page publishers in 1900.

this winter, and I never could take language lessons[8] or attend Columbia University lectures from out there. And, as for society, I think we should have very little of it.

Wednesday, October 24th. Very well. Warm day.

We went about eleven a.m. with the Doubledays to look at a house in Tenth Street, which they thought we might like.

The house is perfect. The rooms are large, light, and well furnished.

If the owners will only bring the price down to within our means!

I was horribly tired when I got home and had intended lying down with a book the entire afternoon. Instead, however, I had to go and see Miss Hesse.[9] She was Cousin Charlie's and Susie's bridesmaid and was consequently devoted to Cousin Charlie and felt his death very much.

We discussed Isa Cabbal's[10] behaviour at the funeral. She was dressed in as deep mourning as Cousin Susy, and made a terrible fuss. The morning of the funeral she had some sort of hysterics, and in them very nearly strangled Cousin Susy.

Thursday, October, 25th. Very bad. Rainy day.

As soon as I began to dress, I began to feel absent-minded, and while I was doing my hair I was really very bad, so I went and told Mamma that I didn't think I would be able to go to the Rogers' to dinner tonight. Then I took off my corsets and lay down on my bed, while Maria sent for my breakfast. While eating my oatmeal I fainted. Whether it was because I had again been overcome with homesickness and various feelings, which I could not restrain even with Maria in the room, at the sight of some violets, or what finally brought on the fainting, I don't know. It came, at all events, and after it I slept and rested until about three o'clock when I had a little soup. When I had finished that meal I got dressed and went to Dr. Helmer. I was kept there a

---

[8] MT claimed that even at age three Jean would argue in "English for light skirmishing, and German for 'business,'" which was natural enough since she had German governesses while the family lived in Germany.

[9] Fanny C. Hesse was Warner's sister-in-law.

[10] Should be Cabell—Isa Carrington Cabell, a Hartford friend of the Warners, wrote *Seen from the Saddle* (1893).

---

good while before he began his treatment, which was very severe today. I have decided to go to the Rogers' dinner.

On my right sat Mr. Cole, May Rogers' husband, and on my left Harry Rogers,[11] with whom I didn't exchange half a dozen words because next to him on the other side sat Miss Benjamin, whom he is going to marry on the seventh of November. I didn't fancy her.

She was altogether too squirmy, noisy and showy-off. From his looks, Harry Rogers seems like a nice boy, but not very deep. He isn't twenty-one yet. I don't know Miss Benjamin's age. May is beautiful. She was dressed a little too low but she is about the most picturesque looking little thing I have seen in a long time.

It doesn't seem possible that she can have been married once before and that they had great difficulty to get her out of it.

She was a mere child at the time and didn't dream that what she thought was simply a game could be a real wedding, and that she could be held to it. The man wanted to, however, and so Mr. Rogers paid him $50,000 to begin with, and sent May to Europe with Mrs. Duff, and then set to work to get a divorce, which he finally succeeded in getting.

Now May is happily married to Mr. Cole and is hard at work getting her house ready. It is up on 72nd Street opposite her sister's.

They tried to make Harry wait and not be married so soon, because they had wanted to have a great celebration of his coming of age in December, but he wouldn't.

The girls call their step-mother "Mother," which I shouldn't think they would, because it can't be so very long since their real mother died, and they surely must be able to remember her.

Mr. Rogers had a hack sent for us, so we drove home in what looked like a private vehicle, in state, and not in a shabby cable car. It was very kind and considerate of Mr. Rogers. We got home very late again. It was already half past eleven.

Friday, October 26th. Very well. Gloomy day.

At breakfast Mamma was very much upset by a letter Clara received from Harmony Twichell, saying that Mr. Dunham thought they had better not dine with us but would come and call during the evening.

---

[11] Mary, 25, and Henry H., Jr, 20, were children of H.H. Rogers, vice-president of Standard Oil, who would be Twain's lifelong friend and financial manager. Mary's husband's name was William Robertson Coe (not Cole). Harry wed Mary Benjamin.

Soon after lunch Mrs. and Miss Davidge called. Mrs. D. was as interesting and attractive as ever, but Miss D. as unattractive as she always was.

Mrs. D. said she had been to see the Shinns[12] and found them living in one large room in which there were only two cots, a bureau and two ordinary chairs. No carpet and none of the ordinary comforts one usually thinks of people having in their houses. This one large room is their bedroom and studio all at once. There were between two and three hundred of Mr. S's pictures in it when Mr. and Mrs. Davidge went there. She liked the pictures immediately and thinks Mr. Shinn is a genius, an uneducated natural genius.

In the evening after dinner Mr. Dunham, Mr. Barney, Uncle Joe and Harmony came to call.

Uncle Joe is the same dear old thing he always was, and what is more he doesn't seem to have changed at all.

Towards the last I had been sitting on my heels in order to be nearer to Uncle Joe and hear him talk. In that way both my feet went to sleep so that in order to rouse them I stamped them somewhat. That annoyed Mamma, who told me to go to my room if I wanted to stamp. I continued for a moment and then stopped. Before I had quite stopped she turned and glared at me, which made me simply boil. I am not an infant and don't choose to be treated like one, certainly not before people. After the visitors had left I said goodnight to Papa and later to Clara but not at all to Mamma and then came to bed where I read for some time in that delightful book, *Bob, The Son of Battle*, by Andrew Ulliphant.

It is one of the most charming stories I have ever read and contains some of the best descriptions and conversations I have ever seen in a book.

Saturday, October 27th. Very well. Somewhat rainy.

Before the morning was over Mamma came and explained some of her methods of speech last night. I daresay I may have been somewhat in the wrong and irritating.

Right after lunch we went with Mrs. Pond[13] and Bim to see *Sam Toy* at Daly's Theater.

---

[12] The realistic painter Everett Shinn is grouped with the Ashcan School.

[13] Martha Glass (Mrs. James B.) Pond was wife of MT's lecture agent who, in 1900, published *Eccentricities of Genius* about life on the lecture circuit.

When we got home we found that Maria had at last arrived.

She left at about eight this morning to meet her sister Anna who was to land from the Campagnia. When the boat got in they had great difficulty getting them to allow Anna to get off. We very foolishly had forgotten to give Maria a paper with papa's nom-de-plume on it and stating that Anna was coming to be our cook.

They had a tragic crossing. One two-year-old child died, and another was born of a husbandless eighteen-year-old girl one day before they landed, and one other was expected to die.

Anna seems very nice but she will have to be taught a few things just as Maria was. Such as not sitting down or rather remaining seated when we are standing talking to her.

While we were still at dinner William Webster's[14] card was brought in. We had him taken upstairs and told that we were still at dinner. Then we arranged that Papa would go up and excuse us, saying that Mamma was very tired, which was true, and would have to be excused.

We had been in Clara's room about two minutes when the Howells' cards were brought. We of course wanted to see them so had them brought up. They rang at the wrong door and when[15] made some remark to that effect I said no, that we had been trying to get rid of someone and so hadn't been in the drawing room.

Mamma went right in, and in a moment I followed, and then in about five minutes Clara did, too. It was rather awkward because it showed so plainly that we hadn't wanted to see him, our own relative, but were willing and glad to see the Howells.

I was unkind enough to leave Willie entirely with Mamma while I stayed with Clara and John. Clara gave John two letters or rather handwritings to read. One was of Ethel Newcomb and the other of Mr. Swahnberg,[16] ça va sans dire. Although absolutely out of practise he really read them both quite well.

---

[14] Son of MT's sister Pamela's daughter, his father had conducted MT's publishing firm, Charles L. Webster & Co., until his death nine years previously.

[15] Besides being son of the leading litterateur William Dean Howells, John at 32 was a good architect who would later design MT's estate, "Stormfield," at Redding, CT.

[16] One of Clara's succession of beaus, he was probably a Swede they met the previous year at Sanna, Sweden, where Jean underwent treatments at Kellgren's Summer Institute.

Clara thought she had given him an entirely Swedish note of Mr. Swahnberg's. After he had left, however, she discovered that a good part of it was English and that it was signed "lovingly yours."

John seemed very much exercised by the fact that Clara could read Swedish. He said he would have nothing more to do with a person who could do that; I wonder what the poor thing will say when he finds that she not only reads and talks a little Swedish but loves and intends to marry a Swede?

Clara felt the same old-time attraction and fascination for John, so that she felt uncomfortable and sort of jumpity about it and him. I felt him so strongly that I spent the night dreaming a composite dream about *Bob, The Son of Battle* and John Howells.

It seems to me that every day I yearn more strongly for the sort of love Clara feels for, and gets from, Mr. Swahnberg. I also get more and more afraid that no one will ever love me. Of course it is perfectly true that I am still very young, but dear me! most girls of twenty have had at least one or two men who have liked them very much indeed, if not really loved them. I know perfectly well that Clara is a very great exception to the general rule. By the time she was my age, five or six men had shown some signs of great affection or friendship for her even if they hadn't said it in so many words. Is it going to be my miserable lot never to really love and be loved, that would be too dreadful and would offer another fair reason for suicide, if as seems likely, Dr. Helmer succeeds in curing me.

Sunday, October 28th. Very well. Dark day.

We are expecting Aunt Pamela[17] today. She is to come between three and four, and we, all of us, dread the visit terribly, Papa most of any. She, poor woman, has an incurable habit of wanting to know it all, which nearly drives Papa mad.

Mamma and Papa went to a six o'clock supper with Mrs. Dodge,[18] from which they didn't return until about eleven. Clara went to a seven o'clock dinner at Norman Hapgood's,[19] from which she didn't

---

[17] MT's 75-year-old sister, Pamela Moffett.

[18] Mary Mapes Dodge, longtime family friend, had been widowed young, raised two children as a professional author, most notably of *Hans Brinker*, and edited *St. Nicholas Magazine* for many years.

[19] Drama critic for *Atlantic Monthly* and other magazines, he had recently been named editor of *Collier's Weekly*.

return until after ten, so I reigned supreme during the evening; which reign I spent in reading *Les Misérables*. Mr. Cushing was at Clara's dinner, dear old-time-Paris-hollow-laughed Mr. Cushing. Clara never thought to ask him to call, but I hope he won't be bashful on that account.

Monday, October 29th. Very well. Beautiful, cool day.

Dr. Helmer quoted the absurdest letter which Dr. Still received once, that I think I ever heard of. *La voilà:*

> "Dr. Still, dear sir:
> Enclosed is one dollar, for which I wish you would write and tell me what is the matter of my wife."

The letter was sent from California and received in Missouri.

The treatment was very painful indeed several times this morning, much more so than it has heretofore been. At one time I feared that I was going to have both Dr. Helmer and his brother at work on me, but Dr. H. apparently didn't find it necessary to have his brother's assistance today.

As usual I lay down right after lunch. I got up at five and for a minute was very absent-minded. It passed off very soon. Soon after I had finished my tea a scrap of paper was brought up bearing the following inscription:

> "Mary J. McKenna.
> I would like to see one of the young ladies for a few minutes."

The handwriting was scratchy and rather like a servant's, and, as I hadn't the faintest idea who it was, I said I would see her.

When Miss McKenna came up she said she had known us by sight in the old days in Hartford and wished to offer us a copy of her book.

She said she had worked in the tenements and had studied the poor question at Miss Dodge's request and instigation. As I hadn't the faintest idea who Miss Dodge might be, I felt decidedly uncomfortable. That wasn't my only reason for not feeling at my ease. I had sort of an instinct or feeling that Miss McKenna was one of the "gentile poor" she had spoken of and had really come to ask for help of some sort.

Just before she left, she said that if we had any work of the kind she did, she would be very glad to do it and then in a whisper:

"I don't suppose you are very likely to have any, because you keep a maid."

She didn't stay long, fortunately, and I hope we may be able to help her in some way sometime, but I rather doubt it. At dinner Mamma said she was sure Papa would die this winter. It made us shudder and gave as her reason—that he was beloved by all that he couldn't possibly live long.

After dinner Miss Pinkham, Clara's agent came to talk some business matters over with her, and they got everything arranged, at least to Clara's satisfaction.[20] They like Miss Pinkham very much, but her underling, whom she didn't bring this time, is horrid.

Thursday, November 1st.

After a terrible amount of packing and general scurrying about, we succeeded in moving after lunch. The house was in a horrible state of confusion after all our trunks and the two pianos had been moved in, but nothing regulated.

The Gilders were kind enough to ask us out to dinner and to supply us with blankets for the night on our return home, as the house hasn't any in it.

Friday, November 2nd. Very bad. Gloomy day.

I fainted the first time about half past ten. I was sitting on the chamber at the time, and, but for Maria,[21] would have fallen in a heap.

Katie[22] arrived during the afternoon. It was really delightful to see her once more. I fainted again about half past six; this time I was on my bed with Maria again by my side.

I wasn't perfectly well even after my second fainting turn, as I usually am.

Sunday, November 4th. Very well. Rather nice.

Poor Anna has a bad sick headache this morning. I hope the plasmon which Clara sent up to her will help her.

---

[20] She was good enough to be taken on in Vienna by the celebrated teacher Theodore Leschetizky, and did make a professional tour in 1908.

[21] Jean's maid.

[22] Katie Leary, a 30-year housekeeper for the family. Her pseudo-autobiography, *A Lifetime with Mark Twain*, was by the novelist Mary Lawton.

We hoped Gabri[23] would come to tea and stay on to dinner, but a previous engagement prevented his doing so. Clara seems to feel his influence over her already. I must say I shall be glad when Mr. Swahnberg gets here, as I think she will feel outside influences less then.

She said she didn't feel as though she could tie herself down for life to any one person, no matter how truly she loved him, because too many other people had such a tremendous effect on her, an effect that a lover or a husband would be jealous of and would not comprehend.

I sincerely hope her music would make these peculiar ideas and symptoms of her not grow and develop any more.

Mr. Howells, but without John, made a short call after dinner.

Monday, November 5th. Very well. Beautiful day.

It is like a spring day out, as warm as possible.

An announcement about Clara's concert singing has just been published in the *Concert Goer*. Clara went to see Miss Pinkham, her manager, this morning and was told by her that Miss P's office has been simply over-run by newspaper reporters inquiring for Clara's address and photograph. The article was only printed on Saturday; the cause of all the rumpus and excitement is the fact that her being Mark Twain's daughter has in some way leaked out and was in the *Concert Goer* too.

Clara didn't want it to become known and Papa was very highly amused at the idea that she thought it could be kept secret; he will be more amused than ever now, when he knows it's out already.

Just after Mamma and Papa arrived about six o'clock, Gabrilowitsch walked in too.

We were delighted to see him, and he was the same dear, old, attractive, charming, gentlemanly fellow he always used to be in Wien. It really is lovely to see him once more. He wasn't able to stay to dinner and was consequently only here a very short time, but, as he is planning to spend the winter in New York, we hope and expect to see a lot of him.

Tuesday, Election Day. Very well. Heavenly Day.

---

[23]Celebrated pianist, Ossip Gabrilowitsch, would wed Clara in October, 1909, at Stormfield with Jean as maid of honor.

I went with Katie, this time to my treatment. Dr. Helmer, as usual, nearly pulled me to pieces, and he seemed to think my bones were wonderfully solid and hard to move. He gave me rather a longer treatment than usual, too.

About nine o'clock a large number of Gilders with Miss Celia Beaux, the artist, and another friend, came in to see if any of us would care to go and see the election "returns" at the City Club, and the crowds in the streets. I didn't especially feel like going, but as no one else did, I accepted. I don't particularly like the Gilders with exception of the son—and him I don't know—because they all seem a little common.

At the City Club the "returns" were received by telegram every few minutes from all over the Union. At one time, New York State not counting "Greater New York" showed 306,000 for the Republicans and 206,000 for the Democrats; and a little bit later, 313,000 for McKinley against 211,000 for Bryan. Bryan doesn't stand much chance.

Wednesday, November 7th. Very well, but tired. Beautiful day.

McKinley is elected! O'Dell is elected Governor of New York State, as against that beast of a Stanchfield.

I carved for a short time before lunch, but, not feeling very well, I couldn't keep up long.

A Mr. Griswold came about six o'clock to see Papa, and, as he said that he had made an appointment to see him at that time, and Papa not being in, I thought I had better see him.

Mr. Griswold is an old gentleman who was on the Quaker City[24] and thought Charles Langdon, whom he saw then, was my brother. I was very absent-minded once, but only once, fortunately. Of course I don't know whether he had spoken to me while I was in my turn or not, but when I came to I felt an undefinable atmosphere which didn't make me feel comfortable any more.

I arranged to have Mr. Griswold come and see Papa at half past eight tonight, so that he could get his answer about the Motauk Club dinner of honor, to which he is invited.

A little after eleven a tremendous thunder-storm broke over New York. The rain simply came down in torrents, and it thundered and lightninged horribly for a long time. The rain poured in at

---

[24] The ship that carried MT on his first trip to Europe, immortalized in *Innocents Abroad*.

my window so that I had to get up and close it. I got my feet and the bottom of my night gown all wet.

I didn't sleep until nearly two.

Friday, November 9th. Pretty well. Cold, windy.

At the treatment today I had two of the Helmers at once. Dr. George Helmer and his short, fat brother. Dr. Helmer stuttered badly when he first began to speak, so that I thought he was making fun of his brother, whom he was introducing. I decided later that he usually keeps his failing wonderfully under control, but that he does occasionally stammer.

Clara came back from visiting Mrs. Baldwin shortly before one o'clock. At lunch-time a lady reporter came from the *Herald* to see her and stayed a perfect age. Altogether, Clara talked two hours with that woman, so that she talked all her voice out of her and had almost none to sing with in Knabe Hall.

While we were still at dinner, Mrs. Frank Cheney was announced, so Papa and Mamma went in to see her. After Clara and I had finished our dinner she went upstairs to write a "billy" and I into the library, where I found Colonel Cheney as well as his wife. They are of course still in deep mourning for their son Ward, who was killed in the Philippines.

We had to leave at nine o'clock and go over to Mrs. Gilder's evening at home or reception, whichever it really was. Pilla and Mr. Howells were both there but to our disappointment John was not.

Mamma thought it very queer that Pilla, who could certainly see for sure that I was "out" and not a child in the nursery, did not ask me for the entertainment to which she had asked Clara for next Sunday afternoon and evening. I think it's horrid of her, and I should think Mr. Howells or John might suggest to her what she should do. Of course I don't expect anything of Mrs. Howells; she never does anything.

Saturday, November 10th. Reasonably well. Cold, glorious day.

When I got downstairs I found that the telegram, which Papa had sent yesterday to Mr. Gillette[25] requesting him to send him two seats and the price for today's matinee, had been answered

---

[25] A Hartford actor financed early in his career by MT, William Gillette was best known for his role as Sherlock Holmes.

by Mr. Gillette's sending Papa a telegram in which he told him that a box had been reserved for him, the charge for which was thirty cents!

We had lunch very early, and then Mamma and I started for the Harlem Opera House in a motor coupe.

I was absent-minded once or possibly twice, en route. We got there a few moments after the curtain had been raised, but Mr. Gillette had not as yet appeared on the stage. The house was packed, there being only three boxes and no seats empty.

Mr. Gillette's entire company was excellent. One or two of the members just a trifle over-did their parts but as a whole it was a wonderfully acted play. Mr. Gillette was *superb*. He was not only superb in his manner, voice, gestures, bearing, enunciation, everything in the art of acting was perfect, but especially his looks. His looks—his beautiful, sad, noble, face and head—were given him by God, and he was merely given the power to improve those looks an infinitesimal amount by shaving off his mustache, and that he has done.

We, or at least I, thought and hoped that we might see Mr. Gillette after the play, if he wasn't able to come into the box between any of the acts. I suppose though that with his having to act again tonight he could not waste any of his strength beforehand.

I hope Mr. Gillette may be able to spare the time to come and see us tomorrow at tea-time.

We found Mildred Holden and some old Western friends of Papa's calling here when we got home. The Fullers[26] were not attractive, and Mildred was the same as she always.

Both Clara and Mamma made me angry at dinner, so I excused myself early and came up to my room. A little later Mamma came up here and without really saying anything I could see that she wished to make up, so I said I might come down at nine-thirty and play cards. I didn't want to a bit. All I wanted to do was to sit still and cry, but I knew that I would not be allowed to remain alone, so after Clara had come in to see about my coming downstairs I finally went.

I am not sorry I did go, because I felt for the time being a trifle less melancholy.

It is dreadful, though, to feel as I so often do. I have no real friends, no talent of any kind, no love, no home or at least no

---

[26] Probably the Frank Fullers, one time secretary of Utah Territory. MT's old pal from Comstock Lode days, he helped Twain considerably when he first came to NYC.

one to live at, and abominable health. If I could only have a real love, a real talent, and a decent sort of health. Clara seems to have so much; she has two great talents, many true friends, and more than enough devoted lovers. Her health is fairly good.

Taken unwell at eleven o'clock.

At about one I dropped asleep, only to waken at three in perfect agony and having had a more than semi-conscious dream, full of ghastly backache and Sherlock Holmes personified by Mr. Gillette. I lay awake in torture for a very long time.

Monday, November 12th. Reasonably well. Gorgeous day.

Mamma went with me to see Dr. Helmer about herself, as well as to speak to him about me.

Mamma told him that I was absent-minded every day now and that before, when I had had two fainting turns in one day, I sometimes went two weeks without being troubled once. Dr. Helmer said that very often in diseases when they had gotten to the root of the evil it would seem to be getting worse. He said he had had one case like mine which grew steadily worse until finally the patient had thirteen fainting turns on one day and then no more. That thirteenth faint was the last one she ever had, at least caused by the disease.

Dr. Helmer examined Mamma when he had finished with me and told her what she already knew, that she had a great deal the matter with her. He went on to say that her acid centers were in very bad condition; they are what cause her gout. Then that her liver wasn't working right and that of course her goiter was a bad one, but that he had cured larger ones than hers. Her collar bones are out of place; they are much too low down; and then of course the tear duct of her left eye has long been out of order and has had several operations. Lately it has begun to materate as well as water, but Dr. Helmer didn't intimate that he would not be able to cure it because of the operations Mamma has had, but neither did he promise to cure it. I imagine that he could not tell for sure until he had given it a treatment or two. He gave her a slight treatment today, and Mamma, I am thankful to say, is going regularly twice a week from now on. We thought that it would perhaps be best for us not to go on the same days, so we are not going to.

We have our new butler, Sherman, at last, and he seems very nice.

We got started for Carnegie Hall a few moments late, but we got there before Gabri had appeared. He had sent us a beautiful big box with plenty of room for six or eight people, so, besides John, we asked Dr. and Mrs. Rice to come and hear him. Papa couldn't go as he had a previous engagement to some sort of a press association sociable.

I think Gabri was called back three times after the concerto before one laurel wreath was taken to the stage. He of course came back a fourth time to get that.

It was a quite large wreath with two long white ribbons on one of which was his name in full: Ossip Gabrilowitsch in gilt letters, and on the other, also in gold letters, the following: "Welcome to America, from the Clemenses."

It was the only wreath he received during the evening, so we were probably the only friends he had in the house.

Everybody applauded wildly, ladies as well as gentlemen; I nearly clapped my hands off. During his many exits to bow to the applause, Gabri bowed right up at our box two or three times. I can't see at all well when I am clapping, so I was obliged to fairly pound my hands together and then hastily pick up either my lorgnettes or my opera-glasses in order to see at all well. During a few of these speedy "snap" glances I saw Gabri turn right toward our box, smile and bow.

My left hand and wrist really ached from clapping. Although I am about as unmusical as anyone can be, I was really and truly carried away by Gabri's playing. I suppose knowing him and being as fond of him as I am may have made some difference, but it can't have been the cause of all my feeling.

As soon as the programme was over and the wild applauding had begun, the people pushed from their seats down to the foot of the stage and stood in great groups and bunches right by the piano—not three feet from Gabri's chair, some of them I think.

He looked perfectly stunning tonight. He always looks more handsome in evening dress, but tonight with his hair a little longer he looked really superb. It was lovely of him to send us so beautiful a box, or any at all for that matter. We went to the green room, which was simply packed and crammed.

We couldn't half get at Gabri there were so many people crowding about him. We of course succeeded in speaking to him, shaking hands with him, and introducing him to the Rices and John. Clara also succeeded in inviting Gabri to come to dinner tomorrow night.

We didn't stay in the green-room long as it was already late and we had invited John to come and help us eat our salad and fruit supper with us.

The Rices came as far as the door with us and as we couldn't all sit together in the car I was fortunate enough to happen to sit next to John; so I held a screamed conversation with him all the way home.

Mrs. Rice had on what I suppose she considers a lovely bonnet, I think it is horrible. It had an entire parrot on it. There was no felt or straw visible, but only the green feathers—head, neck, and all of this poor little parrot. I would as soon go out with a skull and bones on my breast as wear such murderous ornaments as she had on.

Our supper was very good, and after it Clara and I went into the library and drawing room and sort of idled about. Clara was too high-jinkety to sit down and converse. She wanted to dance, but as there was no one to play, she began to play a waltz. John asked me to dance it with him, so we pulled the rugs on the drawing room floor to one side and began.

Clara played her dear old rolling waltz, which I generally can dance with anyone to, but tonight, whether it was too slippery and John doesn't dance quite in time to the music or what the reason may have been, I could not dance at all with him. I kept stepping on him and stubbing his toes; it was dreadful.

Finally Clara played a two step, and that went much better but not perfectly by any means.

Clara said twice in John's hearing that Gabri was a perfect dear and once that she loved him. She thinks that he believes that she is in love with him.

John finally left at about twenty past twelve and carried off Clara's two-ringed heart brooch and left his most valuable key in her hands. I believe he took the pin intentionally but I can't quite make up my mind about whether he really meant to leave the key here or not.

Tuesday, November 13th. Fairly well. Bright day.

Did a little carving in the forenoon, but just as I was about to take a walk with Clara my back began to be troublesome so I stayed in.

Gabri didn't come till nearly dinner time so that after we had talked a while, only just enough time for two songs remained before dinner. Mrs. Warner was here, too, and she of course does not understand German at all. Gabri thought Clara's singing was infinitely better than it used to be in Vienna when Brandt was her teacher. He kept repeating: *"Es ist gar kein Vergleich, gar kein Vergleich!"*

At dinner, which lasted a perfect eternity, Clara and I continued to speak German with Gabri. Mamma turned to me once and said I must speak English because of Mrs. Warner. I tried to and I of course knew and felt that it was inexcusably rude for us to be speaking German when she couldn't understand a word; but Clara kept on speaking German, and a habit is a very stubborn thing to break at once.

Both Papa and Mamma gave Gabri several very decided hints about not speaking German, and he said once that he would not say another German word, but in half a second when he turned to speak to Clara he dropped right into German. It was merely thoughtlessness and interest in what he was saying to Clara, and then, too, he of course speaks German much more easily than he does English.

Mrs. Warner didn't seem to object to his speaking German. She said she liked to hear a language she couldn't understand. Most people would have been furious.

After dinner we three went into the library and had an old-time cozy Vienna talk. It seemed like the old days. Clara told Gabri her—what would make me hopelessly melancholy—views about idealism etc. I don't quite understand what she means, although I have heard her tell her views in English, when she was of course much better able to express them.

I found it very hard indeed to express myself in German, and once I made a most horrible mistake out of which I couldn't seem to pull myself. Fortunately, Clara had just said that she didn't respect him any more since his concert but that she had felt something else more. Gabri turned to me and said: *"Hoffentlich haben Sie mehr Respect seit dem?"*[27]

And I answered: *"Ich habe uberhaupt kein Respekt mehr fur iss Spielen."* Gabri and Clara, of course, howled and I instantly saw what I had done, but, try as I would, I couldn't patch up or in any way change my fool remark.

It was of course entirely due to my having gotten out of practice of speaking German. Clara came to my rescue, and said: *"Du*

---

[27] "Hopefully you have more respect for me since then?" "I have above all more respect for the playing." ... "You mean to say that you have no more respect because of his playing."

wolletest sagen dass du keinen Respekt mehr wegen sein Spielen hattest."
I think he had understood before but I have rarely felt like such
a fool as I did then.

He began to give Clara a very excellent singing lesson so I sat
in the drawing-room pretending to read.

At one time when Clara had gone up to get some more music,
he came and spoke to me for a few minutes.

He seemed very much surprised to find me still reading *Les Misérables*, because he remembered my having received it in Sweden. I
then said that I could not remember the first part of the book at all.
He of course howled at that asigre U concequesimesunry Serasur
mo meure scume asorime my scabusive makerie apounge assopre co
rouse asigre mxamre asigre my geceace moremxepr xagre a Scorumem
punsiegre my memopy.[28] I am not sure whether he altogether believed
me or not, but, as Clara came down then, I could not continue,
which is perhaps as well. I asked him not to mention what I had
said and I know that he is absolutely trustworthy.

Clara asked him what we had been talking about and he answered:
"Ihr schlechtes Gedachtnis."[29] She said nothing more and I don't think
she is ever likely to think of it again.

The papers spoke disgustingly about the concert. They are
positively revolting.

Papa seems to be planning to dictate his work to me and to
have me write it on a type-writer. He is really going to speak to
the Harpers about the price of a good cheap type-writer and to
Miss Harrison Mr. Rogers' secretary, too.

I didn't sleep till after two I was so *aufgeregt bei Gabri.*

Thursday, November 15th. Very well. Cold and bright.

Mr. Swahnberg's last day at Eaton Square.

As a box has been sent us for a matinee this afternoon, I went
with Papa. He had to go out of courtesy to the actress, and sender
of the box.

I think Papa enjoyed the play—he seemed to. I know he enjoyed
Annie Russell[30] and the Cardinal. He was an old dear and such
a sinner.

---

[28] Coded passage: as a consequence of my absentmindedness in having received such
a precious gift. As soon as it came my disease made me forget it had come, proving
very annoying.

[29] "Your bad memory."

[30] British-born ingenue who would later star in Shaw's *Major Barbara*.

There are two blizzards raging out West, and, as it is very cold here and the cold seems to be increasing, we may have reason to believe that cold weather and possibly snow is approaching.

Mr. Runey brought a carriage to take us—Papa, Mamma and I—to the reception at Delmonico's Inn. The reception was given by the "Association of American Authors," of which association Papa is not a member for the very good reason that he doesn't wish to be. Most of the members are people who have written insignificant little articles, either in some rather poor magazine or monthly or weekly paper, and consequently desire to be considered authors.

I wrote to Mrs. Rice and asked how we should dress, and she sent back word that she thought evening dress was the correct thing. We found however that no one was as much dressed as we. One lady, Miss Blake, had on a slightly open-necked dress, and her mother may have had the same sort of costume on, but, with the exception of one individual who I suppose considers herself a singer, we were the only ladies in evening dress. Why ladies should wear hats and ordinary worsted dresses when the gentlemen are in full evening dress is more than I can understand.

Most of the people who were presented to us were extremely uninteresting and rather verging on the common. They weren't vulgar at all, but neither were they refined. A Miss Stoddard nearly drove me wild. She is one of those shiny would-be extra sweet and lovely people who haven't any more to them than an underbred puppy. Not as much really, because a mongrel puppy has at least the quality of being amusing.

We came home reasonably early, and a mighty good thing it was too.

Friday, November 16th. Very well. Cold, beautiful.

Mr. Swahnberg goes to Paris to visit a friend for a few days, instead of to Sweden as I thought.

Dr. Helmer gave me pretty violent treatment today.

As Mamma was in another room getting ready, he took the opportunity—since there was no maid about—of asking me about that old habit of mine. It has been so entirely out of my thoughts for so long that I really didn't know what he meant for a second or so when it flashed across me. He said there were still symptoms of that old difficulty in my back, and when I asked him if that could be still affecting my memory he said that it most decidedly could and doubtless was, quite as much as the bromide.

I like Dr. Helmer immensely and feel no end of confidence in him.

Saturday, November 17th. Very well (that is fairly so). Coldish.

Although it's not as cold as it was yesterday, we have had the furnace fire started, and at present (about noon) instead of sending heat through the house, it amuses itself with making us a present of some soft coal fumes.

I took Papa's Klondike gold nugget to be made into a stick-pin for Mamma, at Tiffany's.

Several of Clara's friends came early in order to hear her sing before tea. She had a sore throat this morning. After we had all finished tea, and I had had time to spill a cup down the front of my dress and change the skirt I had on for another one—which didn't all match the waist—Mr. and Mrs. Archie Welsh came in. I nearly suffocated all the evening; the dry hot air from the furnace is very distressing. My cheeks burn as though I had been out on the sea in a very strong wind.

Monday, November 19th. Well. Summer day. Hot.

Maria and I had a "treat" on the way home from Dr. Helmer's. We went into a drug-store and had some ice-cream soda water. It is the first I have had since we landed, and I never had any real soda-water anywhere abroad.

Uncle Charlie was here for lunch. Some of his views and notions irritate me frightfully, but when I am with him he always seems charming.

Poor old Maria Korner Benkwitz wants to see us all. I hope she isn't poor and in need of money.

Just as we were about half way through dinner, who should be announced but Amy Robinson[31] and her father! Just a short time before, Uncle Charlie had said that Amy was living somewhere in W. 10th St. Papa went right in to see them and I followed very soon. She is quite pretty although she has a huge nose and is very short. If one were to see her in Vienna one would swear she was a Jewess. As soon as Mamma and Clara came in, she began

---

[31] Amy is probably the daughter of MT's old billiards' pal from Elmira, George M. Robinson, furniture manufacturer and undertaker.

---

to put on more airs and graces than I have seen for a long time; indeed I have rarely seen such affectation; it was intolerable.

We of course talked about a good many of the girls, and the teachers we used to have at Park Place.

Amy pretends to be studying singing whenever she comes down to New York, and is taking lessons regularly in Elmira. I hope not to hear her when I go up to Elmira for Christmas, as I can just imagine what her singing would be like.

Her father is positively disgusting, sickening, he is so repulsive personally. Papa nearly went to sleep during the call and Mamma was very nearly made sea-sick by Colonel Robinson's personal attractions, together with some odour there was about him.

Wednesday, November 21st. Well. Dark; warm.

When I say I am well I don't mean that I have gone the entire day without an absent-minded turn, but merely that I have only had a few, and those widely separated.

I carved a little in the forenoon and did some copying for Papa.

After dinner we had an hour and a half's siege with Willie Webster. Thank the Lord he left just before Gabri arrived to practice with Clara. She had not undergone the misery of listening to Willie's lengthy conversation, as she thought it would not be good for her to so soon before singing.

Thursday, November 22nd. Ordinarily well. Cold, bright.

Maria and I went to Dr. Helmer's on the top of a Fifth Avenue bus. It isn't as easy to get up there as it is on a London bus, but the air was glorious when we were once up.

My type-writing machine, a "Remington," arrived this afternoon, and I am fairly aching to begin to learn how to use it. I am to have it for a month, at the end of which they will send us a new one, provided we decide that we want to buy one. They are rather expensive, but I think Papa intends to.

Friday, November 23rd. Very bad. Nice day.

As soon as I began to dress, I commenced feeling bad, so I took off my corsets and lay down. Later on, I felt very well, so that when Papa said he thought Mr. Carey could show me how to use the type-writer, I jumped at the chance. As soon as he came

---

up, I was a little troubled, but Katie doesn't think he noticed it, and at any rate I learned how to use it.

I fainted about half an hour after he left. In the afternoon I slept, as I always do after fainting.

Mr. Carey came back to dinner and then took us up to see Francis Wilson in *The Monks of Malabar* at the Harlem Opera House. We went up there in a cable car. Before we had been in it long, who should come and shake hands with Mr. Carey and Papa but John Drew!![32] He then turned around and spoke to Mamma and Clara, the former of course introduced him to me. Mamma asked him to call, and, as he asked where we lived, and doesn't live very far away from us himself, it looks as though there might be a possibility of his coming. He was very attractive and good looking, even off the stage. I do hope he'll come.

Mr. Carey left us at 58th St., but the car-conductor, recognizing Papa, put us off at Tenth Street without being told to do so.

Sunday, November 25th. Well. Pouring.

Glued the chair Mr. Erdal broke. Then studied Russian for nearly an hour. I mean to do one lesson each day (that I am well, of course), until I succeed in finding a teacher, which I certainly mean to try and do.

Mr. Bigelow[33] called this morning. He has one of his daughters with him and is under orders to return to England by Christmas, or be divorced, and he is engaged for several lectures here before January, so he says he doesn't know what to do.

Monday, November 26th. Well. Clearing up.

We went to Gabri's concert up at Mendelsohn Hall which began a little after three, and lasted till after five.

I have heard Gabri play wonderfully many times, but I don't think I ever heard him play as he played today. It was perfectly wonderful!

The hall was very nearly full, and the treat was something perfectly indescribable! We went in behind and shook hands with Gabri, but there was a large crowd there, and we were in a terrible

---

[32] A longtime friend of MT, sired one of America's most celebrated theatrical families, which included John Barrymore and siblings.

[33] A British pal of MT's, Poulteny Bigelow was the one who introduced him to Dr. Kellgren's clinic a year before.

hurry, as some perfectly strange English people had been asked to come to tea at five, and it was already long past that hour.

We rushed home and found our guests still waiting for us. They were Mr. and Mrs. Lee-Hunt, out for Corea. They came to see if Papa wouldn't make a trip out to Corea next summer, see Hawaii and Japan en route and China on the way back. Mr. Hunt has some very fine position in some mines out there, and he thought Papa would get the material for a book and add ten years to his life. He says it is a beautiful trip and the camping out is delightful.

I don't imagine there is much likelihood of our going, unless I should get well between now and the time necessary for starting.

Tuesday, November 27th. Well. Wet.

Mamma asked Dr. Helmer about going to balls, and he said that I mustn't! He said that if I could go and dance for an hour and then come home and go to sleep that it would do more good than harm, but that I must not go and dance all night as the custom of course is. I am perfectly miserable over it, as Dr. Freeland only said last night that he was going to send me an invitation for a ball on the fourth of December, which promised to be a very agreeable one.

Papa has gout rather badly, but when he heard me jump upstairs, I was cussing my luck to Katie, he came right up to see if I had fainted. Poor little lame man.

Mamma likes her feather fan, which Clara and I gave her, very much. She seems to think it's quite a wonder.

Both Mr. Howells and Mrs. Bigelow consider the Blickensderfer type-writer the best, and Papa consequently went and bought one, and we will send back the Remington I have been practising on. The new one is a nice-looking little machine and much easier to carry about than the other. The man is coming tomorrow to teach us how to use it.

IMPROVING MY AVERAGE / Kate Wheeler

T HE PROP PLANE LABORED up the Andes' blue and white spine, at the mercy of blasts and vacuums. My scrambled eggs jittered in their dish, like the coarse yellow foam that storms leave on a beach. I had no intention of eating them: I was counting cities on my fingers, dividing in my head. After calculating backwards twice, I'd just gotten it straight. Being twelve years old, having lived in eight places, I'd inhabited each location of my childhood for one and four-eighths years, eighteen months, too long.

When I'd arrived where we were now leaving, I was seven and had lived in seven places. I'd been in a state of perfect balance, I now realized, like the Golden Age of Pericles: I couldn't remember having worried about anything. But then my dad's company kept him five years in Terremotos, Perú. In the yellow desert of the north, I grew old enough for first loves—skinny Mike Grady, who could walk on his knees in lotus pose, and the Pacific Ocean, which almost claimed me one day in an undertow. Time stretched out so long in Terremotos, I forgot it was dragging me toward this, the day of departure.

Now we were moving to Cartagena, Colombia, on the bathtub-shallow Caribbean. My father's company had promoted him to manage a plant that extruded polyethylene. I'd be able to see Plasticos Revo across the bay from my own balcony, promised my mother, who'd made a househunting trip a month ago and rented the same house my father's predecessor had lived in.

"I hope we leave it soon," I said meanly when she showed me the picture of the house, pink and modern, with a rubber tree over the garage.

"You jackal, I worked so hard," she said, and burst into tears.

"Eat those eggs," she told me now. "A protein breakfast is the best gift you can give your brain."

Before I could hesitate, my father's eye rolled over onto me, and I heard him clear his throat. "Lila."

I stabbed them, wishing I could throw them out the sealed window for condors to eat.

The plane's silver wing hung over the Cordillera Blanca, perfectly static, as if we weren't really moving. If we crashed, I'd touch snow for the first time. I imagined search parties of *cholos* fanning out over a glacier, chewing coca leaves for endurance. By the time they found us, most of the passengers would be frozen, dreaming their way deeper and deeper into total darkness. Not me—I'd read in Jack London how to bury yourself in a drift and remain alive, insulated by snow itself.

Incas' descendants would adopt me; I'd live the rest of my life on the altiplano, playing a *quena* among stone ruins.

We landed, and Cartagena clapped itself around us like a boiled towel. The Customs official smirked as he ran his hands under my mother's nighties, examined the soles of my U.S.—made saddle shoes for marks of use. He envied us, I knew. Still, I wanted to explain that I'd been born in the jungle in Venezuela, and so wasn't blood-connected with this mortifying mountain of imported goods. Because our main shipment wasn't due for several months, my mother had packed everything from aspirin to bedspreads in fifteen suitcases.

My father's new driver took charge of us outside Customs. His name was Cosme Leña. He was the color of a plum and had no voice, only a kind of hiccup like the catch between sobs. As he gesticulated at the porters, my mother explained that Cosme had had a tracheotomy, and so lacked vocal cords. The operation was performed on the HOPE ship, a fact Cosme was proud of, my mom said, with a minuscule lifting of her eyebrows. I saw the scar in the pit of his throat, darker-purple, thickened skin, like a splash of glaze on ceramic.

Mom and I squeezed in back with five suitcases. Cosme babied the company Fairlane along ruts, through ponds, the thin circle of the wheel stopping then spinning in his big hands. Most of the other cars were sturdier, Jeeps or pickups; I'd have preferred one of them, by far, to our fragile U.S. product.

YANQUI GO HOME, all the walls said.

Cosme hiccupped steadily to my father, and bit by bit I deciphered his words of pure breath. He was trying to get his daughter hired as a maid in our house. She was good, clean, hardworking, religious—a Protestant converted by missionaries from the States, Cosme said, as if this were a bond my father must acknowledge. Alas, Señora Leña had just had their eighth baby, and there was no more room in their humble home. So Estrellita, the oldest at seventeen, must leave.

"*Lo pienso, Leña,*" my father said irritably. I'll think about it.

"Po'a'o," Cosme begged. Please.

We rolled past mildewed coral battlements hung with faded wash. Naked boys pranced, an inky cloud hung over the sea, a white goat was staked at the edge of a soccer field. These new sights made me feel I could be happy here.

"There's your school," my father said as we passed a yellow building.

Our house was pinker than its photo. Meters from the bay, its yard was pitted with land crabs' holes. A young woman stood on the front-door porch, a nylon shopping bag at her feet.

"Uh-oh," I said.

"Who's that?" said my mother, who didn't speak enough Spanish to have deciphered Cosme's proposal.

"I think it's our new maid," I whispered.

She came tilting toward the car. Something was wrong with her, too: her right calf was thinner than her left, and gave her walk a crooked kind of eagerness, the limp throwing her body forward on every other step. She stopped in the shade of the rubber tree and stood there trying to look eligible. I shrank down as my father growled in his throat, preparing to dispel her.

"Polio," pronounced my mother.

"E'm'ia," Cosme corrected. *Es mi hija,* she's my daughter.

"Oh, hell, Leña," my father said. "What's she doing here?"

Not polio, Cosme was saying, only a problem of the knee.

"She looks nice," I said, meaning beautiful. Estrellita was the color of a bay horse, with an aquiline nose that made her look like she should be riding on a palanquin.

My father surged out of the car, followed by my mother and Cosme. I slid farther down in the seat and ran my fingernail down the vinyl's textured stripes. When their voices stopped I mustered courage to sit up, terrified I'd see Estrellita prostrate and kissing my father's wingtips, or else humping to the bus stop with her sad bag. But all had been resolved; Estrellita Leña was ours. She was following my dad to the front door; he strode ahead holding the key in front of him like the solution to great problems. Cosme was thanking my mother, clasping his hands and rolling his eyeballs skyward.

My mother nodded sideways for him to start unloading.

"Well, we got a bargain," she said wearily. Inside, she threw herself down on a couch the Martins had left. My mother did not always seem strong enough for her own life.

That night I lay on a buttony, damp-smelling mattress between my favorite sheets. They'd been hanging out on a line this morning and still smelled seared by Terremotos' perpetual sun, but I was far from fooled. Outside, blue and orange crabs circled under the porch light, bubbles clicking from their furry sectioned mouths.

I'd recalculated my life on paper, and happily found that my average went down to sixteen months the minute we landed in Cartagena. As I lay in bed it occurred to me that the new maid had acquired an average, too, this very day. After seventeen years in one house, her life was cut in half by moving in with us. Since for myself I did not calculate changes of house in one city, her case allowed me to savor my own magnanimity.

The next morning I peeked into Estrellita's room while she was washing walls upstairs. It was freshly painted chalk yellow, but had a slick cement floor that sloped to a central drain. A pair of pointy white church pumps sat under the bed, deformed to the different widths of Estrellita's feet. She also owned a bottle of perfume, a transistor radio, and a hairbrush. My favorite was the picture tucked into the edge of the mirror. Sinners in a lake of fire. Their mouths were open screaming for the help of Jesus, who stood smiling on a blue cloud surrounded by cherubs. The cherubs were bodiless babies' heads with wings, more like moths than angels.

School wouldn't start for weeks. I met a boy my age at a welcoming party, Walter Nugent, but he'd just come down from the States and couldn't speak any Spanish, so I wasn't interested in him. He had one good trick, which was to scrunch his face to show forceps dents he'd gotten in his temples, being pulled from the womb in Pittsburgh.

I tried catching lizards in the yard. They were fast and I got only one; its blue neon tail broke off in my hand while its green trunk scuttled into a crab's hole. "Grow another tail," I said, burying the old one under the gladioli.

My head was pounding with the heat. In Terremotos, Mike Grady and I had had a zoo. We charged half a *sol* admission to see my iguana, parakeet and scorpions, plus Mike's dog Muffin (whom we said was a lion), his two dead seasnakes in alcohol, and his father's saltwater aquarium. No one came, but the zoo made us happy, until the iguana opened the cage with its handlike claw and ran away.

I retreated to the shade of my balcony, where a plastic-wicker

Kate Wheeler

chair had been left by the previous renters. Staring across the flat, oily bay at the old city, the port, and the pale scientific turrets of my father's chemical plant, I decided all of life was an illusion of the senses. The raw salt smell of the breeze was just molecules hitting my nose. I'd never touch the turrets of my father's plant, even though I could see them perfectly clearly.

In coming days I learned to put myself in a trance by willing my finger to rise and also to disobey me and lie still. Sometimes it stayed paralyzed even when I seriously tried to move it.

I heard the vacuum cleaner stop. A subtle pressure grew against the back of my head—I was being spied on.

Estrellita.

For two days I pretended not to notice.

The diagonals of her back crisscrossed unevenly as she strolled past me and leaned on the balustrade, lifting her pink heels off her plastic sandals.

"*Bonita la suidá',*" she observed. Pretty city.

"*Muy,*" I said warmly. Very.

She sniffed deeply and fell back on her heels again. I wondered where her thoughts went as she gazed beyond La Popa, the green promontory that bounded the far end of Cartagena. So I asked her.

She shrugged. "*Monte. Finca. Perro rabioso.*" Bush, farm, rabid dog.

I wasn't very surprised when, the next day, she said, "*Ven.*" Come.

I followed her inside, through my own bedroom, out a door that opened from the second floor onto the roof of the garage. She had no trouble hopping onto the waist-high roof of the servants' quarters. We walked to the edge and looked over into a patio nicer than ours. Striped tiles, potted *adorno* and crotons, bentwood rockers, and a green Amazon parrot.

"*Mírala, que blanca,*" Estrellita said. Look how white she is.

"*Verde,*" I disagreed, thinking she meant the parrot.

She tisked and pointed. Higher up. "*Blanca, 'ombé.*"

"*Huy.*" A naked girl was creeping across the floor of the balcony, pale and bumbling as a white puppy. A bamboo screen hid her from all angles except from where we stood.

This was Isis Román, oldest daughter of the Román family. They owned the factory that made five colors of soft drink, red, black, purple, green and orange. Estrellita explained that Isis was sixteen but would never marry because of her mental defect. She'd live all her life as a caterpillar on her parents' balcony.

My mother had mentioned that our neighbors were first cousins: the five important families in Cartagena had pure blood from Spain they couldn't bear to dilute. I tried to explain recessive genes to Estrellita, but she already understood them—God sends bad seeds into the womb to punish parents' sins. Especially, pride. From the fierce look on Estrellita's face, I could tell that Cosme and Señora Leña had already been cast into her private lake of fire. I wondered whether she saw my face there, too, among the unsaved.

Isis Román swiveled her head, rolled sideways, and, moving as slowly as seaweed underwater, displayed her breasts, black bush, and pale underarm tufts. Her gray eyes slipped over us, hot and unfocused as the sky. As her hand crawled down between her legs, a sudden vacuum pulled at my womb and I had to step back from the edge of the roof.

Estrellita said, "*Pobrecita. Ella no sabe na'.*" Poor little thing, she doesn't know anything.

Back on the balcony, I asked Estrellita if she herself was engaged. Or, I added, remembering her bad leg, did Cosme want to keep her close to him?

No! She had a fiancé, she said proudly, a truck mechanic named Americo Velarde. They'd be married next year.

"Handsome?" I asked respectfully.

"No." She smiled. "I am the only one who loves Americo."

I was filled with joy. It was so romantic, like Beauty and the Beast. "Why don't you marry him now? Then you wouldn't have to work for us."

"It's to marry that I have to work," she said, explaining that Americo's parents had asked for a cash payment because their son was marrying a cripple. Cosme didn't like Americo, so Estrellita was earning the money herself. She gave half her wages to her parents, half to Senor and Señora Velarde. She'd be paid up by New Year's.

I was so shocked, my ears rang. "That's not fair," I said. "What about Americo?"

"He is helping."

How could true love accept such a bad bargain? I tried not to think about this, but Estrellita visited my balcony daily and talked about everything, especially love, especially Americo. Americo had called her on the phone while my mother was out shopping. Americo liked green mangoes with salt, and the *cumbia* was his favorite dance. Nothing could ever divide them. The two of them had already become husband and wife to each other, if I understood what that meant.

I said yes.

She made me taste green mangoes, and brought her transistor up to teach me the *cumbia*. We hardly needed music, for in Cartagena an itching syncopation lived in the air itself. On that big balcony we pursued each other, wriggling our shoulders like lovesick pigeons, burning each other's faces with imaginary candles. The *cumbia* imitates a slaves' courtship in ball and chain, dragging one foot behind the other: it was the perfect dance for Estrellita's lame leg.

"*Soy hombre,*" she'd say, grabbing my waist, I'm a man. Looking up at her noble African face, I failed to imagine any future husband. Mike Grady was too far away, and had somehow become too young.

I tried to teach her the alphabet, in its Spanish version with extra ñ and ll, optional y and w. Copying my letters, she gripped the crayon so tightly she nearly crushed it; her letters came out tall and crooked, mauve and lime-green beings with an animated aspect, like the living hieroglyphs of a spell. But these lessons made both of us uncomfortable, and after two lessons we dropped them to return to hotter topics, love, *cumbia*, and the *radionovela* of four o'clock, "*Amores desesperados.*"

The scion of a rich family falls in love with the housemaid. His parents find out and have her locked in a convent, but he comes with a ladder in the night and springs her. They elope, and live in a penthouse in Bogota. The wicked, rich parents try various stratagems to break up their marriage—abduction, the spreading of evil rumors, sending temptresses to the young husband's place of work.

Estrellita listened raptly to this wild plot: I knew she imagined herself in some glittering gown, on a balcony overlooking the winking lights of the capital, and beset by treachery. Alas, I couldn't be the *novia*: I had no poverty, no lover, and no entrapment to be saved from. Instead, I yearned to be the hero. Eighteen and powerful, a rescuer for Estrellita.

Clearly there was no reason why I was I and Estrellita, Estrellita; therefore, no reason for me to be rich and her to be my servant. But, since I found myself in the position of privilege, I was responsible for helping her.

Saving her would not be easy. Having shared their houses with servants for twelve years, my parents never lost sight of their wallets. Our shipment was delayed, too, so there was nothing in the house to steal and sell. Even my piggybank, with its hoard of Peruvian *soles*, was out at sea in some container ship.

I lay awake each night, plotting and worrying. In order to sleep, I put my hand between my own thighs, imitating Isis Román, the girl who didn't know anything. I loved what I felt, but it was embarrassing to imagine sharing such sensations with another person, especially a man.

First day of school at Teddy Roosevelt. I waited for the bus under a banyan tree with Graciela and Adolfo Román, Isis' sister and brother, and Barbara Murphy, a missionary kid with hard red cheeks and a forehead so shiny it looked like her mother must scrub it every day with Ajax.

Graciela and Barbara were both in my grade, seventh. Graciela was three years too old, because she had trouble with English. She wore a tight lavender dress, mourning for a dead uncle, that folded into three creases of her belly. I could see her body was blocky and abundant, just like Isis'. She right away invited me to her *quinceañera* party, a sort of coming out; but visions of nakedness, hers and her sister's, discomfited me so much that I said my parents didn't let me go to boy-girl parties. And added, for good measure, that she looked like a boiled grape, *una uva hervida*.

Barbara sat next to me on the bus. "You better wear shorts underneath," she warned. "Adolfo was lifting up your skirt from behind with his Coca-Cola yoyo. That's what boys at Roosevelt do. Are you saved?"

What a weirdo: I willed her to vanish. "I don't know."

"If you don't know, you're not, and you're going to hell." Lifting her chin, she said, "I'm a half-orphan. My real dad was a martyr."

He'd been murdered by members of a jungle tribe he'd been trying to convert. She told me the story in detail, speaking so fast and smoothly it was like she'd memorized a script. Drunken men locked her and her mother into the kitchen and then dragged her father into the bush and chopped him up with machetes. A bachelor missionary was sent to bring Barbara and her mother down the Magdalena River to safety. This man was now Barbara's stepfather; he was the minister at the *Iglesia Bautista Cuadrangular*.

I left a silence of respect, then said, "That's my maid's church. Do you know Estrellita Leña?"

"Yup," Barbara said, and I realized that she was closer to Estrellita than I was, less of a *norteamericana*—only because she'd lived all her life in this one country of Colombia, I reminded myself. Still, I felt inferior.

I let her sit next to me in class even though it meant I might not make any other friends. She was definitely strange, with that shiny forehead and hard blue eyes glittering with conviction; but a saved half-orphan was a powerful being. In the middle of class she got up from her desk, went to the window, looked out, and returned. Mr. Clements frowned, but kept writing on the board about capitalization. Inspired, after recess I raised my hand and asked to go to the bathroom even though I didn't need to. Of course, Mr. Clements had to say yes.

Liberation.

Walking down the breezeway, I looked into the classrooms at the diligent teachers and distracted students, then outward, past the rattling palms, to where a ball of light hung over the green sea.

I wanted to be Barbara. After school, she invited me to the sea wall to look at the black iguanas, and then to ride home together on the public bus. My mother wouldn't mind; in those days Cartagena was as safe as a bathtub.

"Stay away from the edge," Barbara warned. "A barracuda once jumped out and bit off a woman's foot near here."

We admired the iguanas, wet with spray, lying so still and ancient on the reddish coral blocks.

"How do you get saved?" I asked.

"Just ask Christ Jesus into your heart. Knock and it shall be opened."

At home, I lay on my bed with the air conditioner off, so as not to have distracting noise. My heart beat against my ribs, maybe the Lord trying to get in. "Come in," I said, but didn't feel improved. "Give me a sign if I am saved."

Silence pulsed, thick and heavy. Then I heard Estrellita coming upstairs, whistling through her teeth. I'd forgotten about her since this morning. If I'm saved she'll open the door and say hello, I thought, but she passed by.

Maybe, being already saved, she didn't really need me.

I lay there ten minutes before going to find her, down in the patio combing her stiff redbrown hair. She asked me how school was. I said, "Boring. The daughter of Reverend Murphy is in my class."

"*La Barbara*," Estrellita said, which also means "The Barbarian." I laughed, traitorously.

The next day at school I confessed to Barbara that my conversion hadn't worked.

"You can't throw off sin by your own strength," Barbara explained. "You better come to church."

My mother gave permission easily, saying church would be good for me. "It'll help you think of something larger than yourself." I wanted to tell her I was always thinking about larger things, but I didn't want to sound vain.

I spent Saturday night at Barbara's. The Murphys lived in a converted garage; their biggest possession was an upright piano Eve Murphy pounded out hymns on. No other music was allowed in their home, a fact Barbara was proud of.

I hated Reverend Murphy right away. He was a tall, fat, pale, ugly man who made Barbara and me call him Sir. He stared at me through Eve's Grace as if trying to force my soul into submission; then between bites of meatloaf he asked if I'd ever been to church.

That night, Barbara started teaching me the books of the bible. When I memorized them all I could win a New Testament. The books had a rhythm, like the alphabet's, that could underpin your life: that night, I got as far as Habakkuk.

I asked Barbara what God's view of stealing was, if the stealing was in a good cause—for example, to raise money for a Christian wedding—and I described Estrellita's marriage problem. Barbara said I'd be doing my parents a favor. Wealth turned people into camels, too fat to fit through the eye of Heaven's needle.

In the morning we burst out of the bedroom in pajamas and grilled her mother about breakfast food. "Who made this banana? Who made this egg?"

"Why, God, of course. Silly girls." She was wearing a printed smock that tied down the back, like a hospital gown; her eyes were as mournful as a Cocker Spaniel's, and her secret shone out, plain: she'd loved her first husband, the martyr, but she didn't love the Reverend Murphy.

I heard thunder in the distance as Barbara and I sat down and ate eggs, bananas and toast.

The *Iglesia* was in a humble part of town. Plastic shelf lining had been glued to the windowpanes to imitate stained glass; the bright red, green and yellow light made the room feel even hotter than it was that day, which was still and moist, waiting to storm. The whole congregation was black except the Murphys and me;

patches of color glinted on their sweaty chins and cheeks, and shone around their eyes.

Estrellita and Americo had saved seats in the front row for Barbara and me. Americo was less ugly than I'd imagined. But I was disappointed for my vague ideas about him to be shrunk into any single, unexpected form. He was a pale-brown person, shorter than Estrellita, and solid as a pot. His hand rested on the small of her back as lightly as a dove in its nest; when he and Estrellita caught each other's eyes, a kind of light appeared between them, so that I knew that I was really seeing it—two people in love—for the first time.

Why was I not happy? I couldn't even understand where the light was coming from; they were just two ordinary people.

The sermon was about Jonah and the whale. Barbara's stepfather searched the world's oceans with glittering eyes, he stabbed the air with a forefinger to make his point: God's will is a whale that will swallow us if we resist. His pale, wetted hair straggled like seaweed across his noggin. Outside thunder was rumbling. God's voice, the voice of the reason for everything.

The congregation was moaning, "Si, señor," ominously as the sea. In back a woman started speaking loudly in tongues: Ashmada, Yoi, Verrabazal! A jumping lightness attacked my ankles, bounced up my thighs into my chest; I was nearly lifted from the ground.

Barbara said excitedly, "Feel the spirit?"

"Make your heart open to Christ," the Reverend Murphy cried. "Humbly say Please, Please, Lord."

I was shaking all over. On both sides, my girl friends squeezed my arms, wanting me to be one with them in Christ.

"Please, Please, Lord," I cried, really trying to open my heart.

"Come down," the Reverend Murphy said. "Come down." I got up and joined a little file of people who were being converted. The aisle was a tunnel; at the end stood the Reverend Murphy with his arms upraised. When it was my turn, he put his hands on the top of my head and prayed for my new life in Christ. His touch made me cringe.

The rain started outside, a sudden heavy rush that dimmed the light inside the church. Behind me the congregation sang, the collection plates began to pass around.

Dear God, I prayed, thank you for saving me. Please help Estrellita and Americo. I couldn't feel anything, or anyone, listening, but I kept on praying anyway.

Some weeks later the principal came to class to announce that the HOPE ship was on its way back around the coast of South America, and would stop again in Cartagena before returning to the United States. Roosevelt students were invited to tour the ship and meet the doctors and nurses.

Desk to desk, Barbara and I made faces at each other. As Christian girls, we were entitled to despise all worldly, adult, pretentious and American things. We called the principal "Caesar" and the school "Babylon"; we stopped people in the street to ask if they believed God made the universe. Of course, everyone said Yes: Colombia is a Catholic country.

At home, I asked my parents if they'd heard about the HOPE ship's return. They had, but were not excited either. They were having their Scotches in the living room.

My mom said, "JFK is too handsome to be trusted."

My father huffed, "He's offending the Latins with his largesse. They hate to feel we're better than they are."

"I'm going to tour the ship and meet the doctors and nurses," I said.

My mother said quickly, "Congratulations! It's a *good* ship. Saved Cosme from throat cancer. God knows why he still smokes cigars."

"He likes them," my father said.

They let me make them second Scotches.

"Cosme's agitating to get his daughter's leg fixed on the ship," my father reported. "I don't know if he can."

"I thought they tried to stick to life and death," my mother said.

"He wants me to make a recommendation," my father said, "for the surgery list."

"Oh, do it, Daddy. Then she can get married." I explained the uses of Estrellita's salary, the payoff to Americo's parents.

"Now that stinks," my father said. "Cosme makes enough money. Revo's the best employer in town. I ought to fire him. That old rat. That old weasel."

"Firing him would only make it worse," my mother said. "It's no skin off your nose, honey. One phone call."

"I'd better ignore the whole thing," my father muttered. "It's not ethical. The company wouldn't like it."

"That poor child," said my mother.

"Daddy, please," I said. "Ple-e-e-ase."

"Oh, hell," my father said, meaning yes. I kissed him extravagantly; at bedtime I modified my prayers, no longer begging God to find money for Estrellita, but to guarantee all the linked events that would get her into surgery.

The HOPE ship was huge, white as a sail by day, lit up festively at night, with its name all in capitals written on both sides. Estrellita spotted it sailing into port while I was at school; she compared it to a nurse's hat. She told me the story of Cosme's operation, how he'd been full of tubes and said *barbaridades* coming out of the anesthetic.

She was sitting on a chair in the patio, peeling yucca and putting it into an enamel bowl.

"I'm going to tour the HOPE ship," I said, gritting my teeth against Estrellita's disappointment.

"I'm going to tour it, too," she said.

"What?"

She turned her sharp profile to me and shrugged. Her lips curved up slightly, in triumph.

"Come on," I coaxed.

"They're going to cure my knee."

"*¡Qué bien!*" I gushed. "I was praying for you every night." Maybe I was, then, really saved, and God had heard me in some way; I'd understand after I died.

"Americo was praying, too. I owe it to you two."

"And to the *Padre Todopoderoso*," I said, the All-Powerful Father.

Our eyes shone into each other's. No more bad bargains.

"The truth, I'm afraid," she said. She held her two legs out for comparison, then kicked her right heel against the floor. "It's not so bad. I came out of my mother feet first, that's all. I keep thinking about the scalpel. So sharp." She shuddered. "So much blood."

"Don't worry, you'll be asleep when they do it," I said. "Let's go look at Isis."

Today Isis was dressed in a little sunsuit. When her eyes rolled upward, I waved and jumped up and down to catch her attention. Isis saw, and was intrigued. She sat up and began shaking her wrists excitedly. Then she began hooting like a chimpanzee. Estrellita and I ran away, giggling, just in time to avoid being seen by the Román's maid.

On the day we toured the HOPE ship, Cosme drove me to school. He was grateful to John F. Kennedy, who had saved his life and now was going to remove his daughter's defect. He was grateful to the people of the United States, and to my father, a powerful man, as I must know.

I pretended ignorance. "My father helped you?"

Oh yes. It had been difficult because Estrellita had no grave condition, but Cosme worked for the manager of Plasticos Revo and now Estrellita would be perfect for her new husband. *"E'te'de?"* he said, looking at me with complicity and pride. *Entiende,* do you understand?

I said I understood. "Americo Velarde will love her even more, if that is possible."

Cosme's face clouded. Americo, Americo was a little Indian. Cosme knew a young man who worked for a bank downtown.

"But Estrellita loves Americo," I cried.

Yes, but Estrellita was silly, she didn't know. Now she was saying she was afraid of the knife.

His chuckle axed through all warmth, all confidence. Violently I wished I'd never asked God to get Estrellita on the surgery list. Please, God, forget it, get her off it again, I prayed. Then I realized that I should make prayers general. God might be angry with me for changing my mind. You never knew what might come along with the satisfaction of a specific request.

Please, God, just make it turn out all right.

"Don't make her get the operation," I pleaded with Cosme. "She's beautiful as she is. She works all day, she can dance the *cumbia,* and her children won't be affected."

Silence. Cosme's wide, crumpled baby face was closed up tightly.

The HOPE nurses turned our tongues green with Kool-Aid from the States, the captain showed us the seven layers of paint that lay like icing on all surfaces, and Barbara was hilarious, but I hardly noticed. I had an attack of claustrophobia in the operating room, far below the waterline and inescapable as a tomb. Mr. Clements said seasickness was impossible in port, but still a nurse took me out on deck, where I hung over the railing looking down at the greasy rainbows in Cartagena Bay.

There was no God, really, I thought. Whenever I tried to find him, there was just a hollow feeling at the base of my skull. How could God let the bay get so polluted? How could He let that poor dog die and be floating, rotting, with its entrails coming out? I'd set evil in motion by pretending to believe in Him. If I'd believed perfectly, my prayers would have been answered perfectly. But I'd prayed selfishly, just to get what I wanted, and I'd lied to Barbara about feeling at home in Christ. So anything bad was going to be my fault.

At home, I couldn't find Estrellita. I searched frantically, upstairs and down, in the kitchen and in her room, out on my balcony, and at the Isis-spying place. The cook didn't know, Cosme smoking a cigar in the garage didn't know, my mother didn't know where she was.

An hour later she came in, beaming. She'd been to the little store to buy milk—and! Her voice dropped to a whisper. She'd had a secret meeting with Americo Velarde to talk about her operation, which would be in two days.

Americo was happy that her leg would be fixed. He'd convinced his parents to return some of the money, so now he and Estrellita were thinking about a little house. He told her not to be afraid of the scalpel. He would pray for her all through the operation.

"No," I said. "Your father said he's going to make you marry some bank clerk. Forget the operation—run away and marry Americo!"

I saw Estrellita and Americo flying out over the ocean, holding hands, dressed in white baptismal robes.

She looked surprised. "Don't worry, my father can't make me do anything I don't want to do. I will never marry Ermincio Bastos, certainly not." Her voice dropped. "I can tell all the world, without any shame, that Americo and I have already consummated our union. Then Ermincio Bastos will not want me."

"Yes. How beautiful," I said, somewhat relieved.

"Yes, it was very beautiful." Her smile went inward, like a cat's.

I got up early the next morning to say goodbye and wish her well, but Estrellita was gone. The Fairlane was gone, too: Cosme must have gotten permission to drive his daughter to the ship, and to visit Señora Leña on the way.

I went into Estrellita's little room and sat on the bed. It was just the same as when I'd first peeked into it, except that there was a sharp smell of her recently sleeping body, and the faces of the sinners in her lake of fire seemed mysteriously fewer. It was the coolest hour of the day; a mist redolent of salt and dead dogs rose from the bay and curled into the courtyard.

I sent out my most powerful wish, for it to be my first day in Cartagena again, without anything having happened yet.

All day at school I wished for the operation's success. Not to God, just to whatever there was. Even if there was just a big nothing, I still couldn't help but wish. I asked Barbara to pray, and she did, in Jesus' name.

"We have to have a talk," my mother said the next night.

Her tone of voice told me all but the location: my average was about to improve. I divided quickly. One and three-ninths years. A year and four months.

"Your father's been promoted and we're moving to Bogotá after Christmas. He'll be director of marketing for Venezuela, Colombia and Perú. They haven't named his successor, so don't tell your friends. Isn't it exciting?"

"We'll miss Estrellita's wedding," I said.

"Well," my mother said and sighed. Snakes began to crawl inside my chest. Snakes and worms. My mother's eyes shifted. "You'd better talk to your father."

This was how punishments always began. I approached my father's huge knees. He was reading papers in the Danish chair. "Dad."

He looked up and when he saw it was me, he took off his reading glasses. Presbyopic is the word: he couldn't see small things near him.

When my father spoke, I knew I'd heard the news before, in a dream or in a previous life.

"Honey, there was a problem with the maid's operation." He sounded annoyed.

"We'll miss Estrellita's wedding," I said.

"Well," my mother said and sighed. Snakes began to crawl inside my chest.

A Colombian medical student had performed the operation, not the American surgeon. The student had botched the work so that Estrellita's leg had had to be amputated at the knee. "Cosme was arrested this morning trying to get on the boat with a pistol to kill the guy," my father said. "But I'll bail him out. And I'm paying for an artificial leg. She'll be all right."

"Is she still getting married?"

"I don't know."

"Can I go to her house?"

"No, honey, I don't think it's a good idea. We'll have her come back and see us before we leave."

Ashamed, tiny, filthy, and depressed, I went out to see Isis, but there was only a blue bath towel lying on the balcony. Looking carefully, I saw the terry flattened, like grass where a cow has slept.

If only I could be like Isis, nothing to do except lie in the sun touching myself, all my life on that same balcony. Isis had no average; thinking about Isis' average was like dividing by zero, or trying to imagine God. If I fell off the roof in front of her, she probably wouldn't understand enough to care.

Barbara came to pick me up for church. She walked through the living room like Shadrach in the fiery furnace, inspecting the turquoise sculptured carpet and the objects my parents had looted, like Conquistadores, from each place we'd lived. These things had just arrived, and soon they would disappear into boxes again. They followed us with touching faithfulness, delayed only because they had no life.

Barbara's stepfather had learned from his congregation that Americo and Estrellita were still engaged. I hadn't told my parents, but after the service at *La Iglesia Bautista Cuadrangular*, the Murphys and I were going to visit Estrellita at home. I'd packed some of my stuffed animals to keep her company during her recovery. surely she'd one day have a baby and need toys for it, too.

So I told myself. But I was horrified, imagining my Teddy sitting on the flat bedclothes where my friend's foot should have been. That morning, I believed that I was evil. I realized I'd never wanted to go to the Leñas' house and see how dark it was, how crowded, Mrs. Leña wringing her hands surrounded by her eight babies—now, with Cosme in jail and Estrellita, I had become a distant stranger.

Every night I'd dreamed about the poor leg living on, a separate life: dancing the *cumbia*, dragging a slave's ball, kicking its heel in the sky, having its own funeral in a coffin drawn by black horses with tufts on their heads, floating in the bay with two dead dogs. When, awake, I tried to think where her leg had gone, something hit me so hard along the top ridge of my head, I couldn't see.

I was glad the Reverend Murphy was coming along to the Leñas', because I had nothing to say. I didn't want to let Estrellita talk to me, either.

She might smile at me bravely, and make it easy for me. She might be glad I came to see her, and then how could I ever leave? How could I bear to know that one day I might be standing on a balcony in Bogotá, like the *novia* in the *radionovela*. Standing there, having forgotten enough about Estrellita, and Americo, and all of Cartagena: forgotten enough to enjoy the lights of the capital spread out at my feet?

Kate Wheeler has appeared in a number of magazines including *Antaeus*, *Threepenny Review*, and *Black Warrior Review*.

JUNGLE GLIDERS / *Roger Weingarten*

I was kneeling with my daughter into a chaos
of frog-shaped jigsaw cutouts guaranteed
to coalesce into animal acrobats that range
the upper levels of South Asian jungles, when,
looking up at the Dragon Lizard's ribs spread
into wings pictured on the box my son,
making bomber sounds, held
over my head, I remembered the roach that fell
out of the fist-sized hole in the ceiling
of my first furnished room, almost
eighteen and kneeling
between your pale
knees in the air, mine dug into the heap
of coats and blankets that covered the concrete
carpet of my basement palace, where
we were struggling for warmth
and pleasure, when the gold-bellied
angel of retribution, like a miniature
landlord, dropped through the punch-drunk
hole in my character, through the onion-scented
fumes from the heater jammed in the window
and landed on your freckle we'd christened
The Third Eye. Watching the impossibly
thin legs, upside-down and flailing,
spinning the hard shell, my jungle-
gliding Paradise Tree Snake slid
out of you into the bedclothes. Your cupped hand
pulled me toward your tongue hovering
between your teeth, like the barely
visible eye of a Red-tailed
Flying Squirrel, as if to will
our privacy and concentration
no matter what. Just as your other
hand splayed across the small
of my lower back nudged
me into you, the insect,
whose family tree had inhabited

every Eden, oasis, every four-star
constellation of food and drink,
righted itself and ran
like three little bodies portaging
an upturned canoe toward the secret
passageway of memory, where
I loved you when I wasn't running
on anger, an adolescent
ground predator, dogfaced
and tracking the family
blood into the trap
of my first poem. Is this
the Flying Lemur of Colugo, my daughter
wondered, reaching
for the upside-down creature, its claws
around a branch, sheltering a smaller
version of itself on its belly, the passenger
staring at the gecko
gliding toward tropical bark, where yellow-flowered
Spider Orchids trail out of ferns, like your hair
between my fingers, while our bodies collided
and turned toward separate futures, and the moonlit
shadow of the jet bearing Kennedy's body
swept a million dreams into the ocean.

STOMPING THE BEAVER PALACE
/ Roger Weingarten

Water flows down the mountain
into a claw foot tub in the cellar,
where I circle a skunk curled up
in the furnace and a half-blind
vole feasting on a plate
of poisoned wheat. Sometimes
the water pipe jutting
out of layers of fieldstone
seizes up in winter, sometimes the World
War II water heater pilot
blows itself out, or I get the urge
to watch the groundthaw in April
purl into the sump pump
buried in the coal-studded floor,
scrape my skull against a square-headed nail
pounded into a beam a century
and a half ago by the farmer who hollowed
out a future in unobliging soil
and aim my flashlight into the crawlspace,
where a predator made a furious meal
of a mourning dove. I crawl in
and twig to how it feels to orbit
a planet in a claustrophobic
tin can or lower myself into a smokestack
with brush and chains. From this eye socket
perch, I press my palm to the light
like a fortuneteller revealing the red-
shadowed future of my bones, turn it off
to see myself in the dark execute
a buck and wing on the mud-and-stick
tiled roof of a beaver palace, then slap
and dive toward the entrance
into the catacomb. Upstairs, and still
bristling at my refusal to attend
courses in synchronized
breathing and belly-dancing,

she spears the blackened remnants
out of the toaster, our child,
upside-down and floating
inside her, ready to scream

DEAR MIKE / *Roger Weingarten*

My half of the closet floor is a sideshow
of shoes I've tucked

into cartons of knickknacks
and clutter, skipping town because

of a job or marriage gone sour
in the cab of a rented truck.

Sometimes, I'll slide
into a boot missing buckles

I wore into Great Uncle Moishe's
secret swamp, his medicine

ball belly chasing
blue-eyed wings, paired

with a wrestling sneaker
I kicked into the bleachers,

where my girlfriend saw my rival
for her affection discreetly ram

his knee into my testicles.
When your estranged daughter phoned,

my wife you never met
hauled me by the feet

out of sleep to relay news
of your heart attack. I pulled the chain

on the closet light, dropped
to my knees and tossed

flapping soles of loafers
over my shoulder, frantic to find

oxblood cordovans—their tongues
twisted into the dry

scream you shipped me off
to college in after throwing

a hook to my chin—trying to sift
through layers of tire-tread

sandals, threadbare walkers, spikes
I never used, gunboats that danced

the hokie-pokie: searching
for a clue to our unresolved

arguments or years of visits terminating
in mutual relief, to the adolescent

joy when I grew
into your spit-shined, tricolor

wingtips. Together,
we stepped into the hushed

nursing home, where Moishe
held my cheeks like the pages

of a prayer book he read
to his flock, who joined him

in chanting "Little Mike"
over and over, embarrassing

us into a silence we grew
accustomed to after my older

brother stepped off the balcony
of his wife's infidelity

into the surf. I held his high-top
running shoes like conch shells

over her ears, until you pulled up
in a brushfire of disbelief and told me

to drop the sneakers and pretend
they never existed. Yesterday,

your wife, cocking her snoot
into the hospital pay phone, said

you remained incommunicado, but if I
wanted to grovel and beg in a letter,

she'd put it in your hands
when the time was right.

I keep going back to
when I was four and zigzagging

a crayon across white
patent leather you were wearing, buried

in the sports page, while Mom
finished dressing for a summer dance.

Your thumbs hooked around suspenders,
holding a smile back, you swore

you'd wear them even if she
didn't approve. When I refused

to apologize, she marched me
off to bed without supper.

I could hear an argument brewing
through the floor until you appeared

to tuck me in, apples and hunks
of cheese falling out of your cummerbund.

When you left the house for good,
you forgot the shoes. Your grandchildren

think of you as a constellation
of anecdotes: driving me to jail

for setting a field on fire; the fart
exploding when I stretched for a pretend

spanking across your lap; the after-dinner
cigar you let me puff until I turned green.

The oldest remembers a man in bathing trunks
who spun him around in an inner tube

until he cried uncle. The youngest,
building a pyramid of shoes in the closet,

wonders if you have a secret hiding place
filled with guns and dynamite.

I don't tell him that every time
I remember the woman

waving a miniature flag
through our old neighborhood—her face

like torn and crumpled paper stopping to scream
at an invisible traitor—and the porchlit

summer night you gave her a glass
of tea she smacked against yours,

the blue numbers on her wrist
visible through the screen door,

every time I imagine you touching
those numbers like a bruise, tucking her

under your arm and rocking
back and forth to music only you could hear,

I want to crash through the screen
of every stranger you helped

---

through a chain of strangers, every intricate
business deal you hinted at,

every brushoff or receiver
hurried into its cradle—crash and land

on a bus to Montreal with you and a bag
of salami sandwiches and tell dumb jokes

and brag until you doze off, then I'll slip
to the floor and weave our shoelaces

together into a knot so complicated,
so tight, you could never untangle it.

Roger Weingarten is the author of seven books of poetry including, most recently, *Infant Bonds of Joy.* He directs the MFA program at Vermont College.

AKI / *Kathryn Burak*

A KI LEANS OVER the steaming bowl. The dashi is the color of
tea. She watches several oil blobs float on the surface, gently
change shape, combine, as she stirs the soup, as she touches her
spoon to the tiny circles of green onion that float to the top. The
steam smells like nothing but heat. She sips from the spoon. It is
without much flavor, but warm, and has an edge of smoke and
metal. The taste after fish. She stares off, distracted by a sudden
movement in the yellow leaves outside the kitchen window. They
will be off the trees soon, she knows.

"You'll get used to it," her father says, a kind of smile at the
edges of his lips. His voice is soft and low. "And I'll get to be a
better chef," he says. She nods back. It is not in the unwinding
sense of absence in the house but in the flavor of the everyday
food she eats that she misses her mother the most, her mother
gone four months.

"It's not bad," she says, but she does not look at him and he
has begun to learn what this means to her. He looks at the top
of her head, her dark hair.

"Ice cream for dessert," he says. "Store bought." Then they
smile at each other, the father clearing the table efficiently.

After dinner, Aki sits in her room, all of her books opened, but
piled on top of one another: History, English, Algebra, Biology.
In order of what she enjoys. History is first.

She notices her face in the mirror across the room. It is a face she
almost does not recognize in this light: eyes, nearly invisible nose,
straight line for lips. It could be her mother's face as it is in her
memory now, a face with indistinct features. She remembers the
sound of her mother, her mother's voice, though, and sometimes
thinks she hears it in another part of the house or outside, beyond
the walls and windows. But the sound is always an animal or a
stranger in the distance along the street, or a pan her father has
dropped.

In the *furo* tub at her grandmother's ranch, soaking, there with
her mother, in the barn in the deep wooden tub, she can remember
her mother's voice was odd, empty as any sound over water.

"They call these hot tubs now," her mother said, her voice bordered with its own echo. "They give them out on the Price is Right."

Her mother sat next to her there in the large wooden tub, the tub big enough for five people to sit in with a bench along the sides. Aki looked around the barn; she can remember doing it: looking at the high ceiling, the hay loft, the person-sized tires on the tractor, looking hard at anything, on purpose. She remembers the water as almost unbearably hot, feeling the water in her throat, lungs, as if it had permeated her skin, was absorbed into her organs, was inside every cell. She waved the water around in front of her to circulate it, to cool it, the current renewing the shock of the heat on her skin all over her body. Through the corner of her eye she could see her mother resting her neck back on the rim of the tub, leaning her head back, closing her eyes— was she resting or giving up, her arms at her sides?

Aki could see the scar near her mother's shoulder, then—a scar, like a patterned ridge, a line of little chew marks running down her left side, that seemed to swallow her left breast. The other breast was round, sort of droopy—normal, with a dark brown nipple: alone it seemed more strange on her mother's body than the missing breast and the long repetition of the stitching that was like a relief map in the skin.

Aki watched the woman as she rested her head back, as the woman ran her fingers from the top of the scar down until the hand disappeared into the steaming water. The daughter looked down into the deep brown dark of the tub, the heat rising through her head.

Now, as Aki stares into the pile of books she can see the scar though it is a map of the path of the Green Mountain Boys. She is not sure, even after thinking about her mother in the Japanese tub, of anything about her mother's face, though she is sure she misses the taste of her mother's food.

"Lunch money?" her father calls from the doorway to her room; he does not look inside.

"I'll be out in a second," she says, packing her books in her knapsack and taking it to the living room where it will be ready for the morning, a habit her mother insisted on since first grade.

When Aki has gone to bed for the night, her father reaches over to put the money in the pocket of her bag as his wife instructed him, the way she would. Soundlessly and gently he lifts his daughter's knapsack onto his lap where he sits on the couch. He puts the folded dollar into the pocket and zips it back, then stops for a moment, looking at the red book bag on his lap. He unzips the large compartment where the books are neatly packed.

He asked his friend, the father of four children, for suggestions on what to discuss with his daughter at dinner. He and his daughter seemed to have nothing to say. "Ask her about her science class," Hamahashi said. "That's what you know. You will have that in common."

So now, he unzips the bag, carefully, as if the contents are liquid and could spill. Thick books, The American Story, Algebra I, Uncovering Life. He puts the others back and leans over the textbook, moving quietly, secretively. He opens the book, turning pages slowly and quietly, avoiding sudden movement. He stops at The Cell, he reads, leafs through the book more. The mitochondria. DNA, good, he thinks, I can talk about DNA... Cell-division— turning pages gently. The human embryo, the zygote, the sperm and the egg. He stops then suddenly, closes the book and puts it gently back into the pack in the same spot on top of the other books, upside down as he remembered it was. The bag smells of pink erasers he can remember from school, and mildew. He makes a mental note: he will have to remember to ask her if she needs to go shopping sometime, for a new book bag or shoes or something else.

Days later, they have steak fried with onions and baked potatoes. Aki tastes the bite of black pepper on the rare meat and the sweet onion. It is a taste she does not care for. She eats slowly, as if in exercise, and is occupied with being done. Her father says things about wind and insulation; she knows he must be thinking of the weather, the cold that's coming. As he cuts his meat, she thinks of how he looks like a potato, how his head is long and oval like a potato, of his dark, ruddy skin. He says, "So, what are you studying?"

"Studying?" She is not sure what the question means.

"In science," her father clarifies. "In your science class." The hard part, he thinks, will be beginning.

"Different things," she says, concentrating on the large piece of meat on her plate, on how to eat the best part soon, on which part is best or even good.

"The Cell?" he asks, quoting the chapter title, thinking his snooping obvious.

"Yes," she says. "Some on the cell, parts of the cell, types of cells." She has a piece of meat in her mouth, shoved to the side of her tongue as she talks. It is tougher meat than she ever remembers eating, and takes a long time to chew.

"DNA?" he asks.

"I think so," she says. "That's coming up in Chapter Eight." She makes it up, guessing. She does not like to look ahead, and rarely does.

"I can help with DNA," he says. "You know that's all I do at work." His voice is clear and certain, a telephone voice, she thinks, one that settles bills, clears up matters. "Here," he says. "I'll get paper. You finished?"

"Oh, yeah. It was a big piece of meat," she says, under her voice. He might not have heard, anyway. He must be interested in getting started.

"You get paper. I'll get a pencil." They clear the table, quickly. Aki can slip the piece of steak from her mouth into her napkin, as she scrapes the dishes. "Just leave them in the sink," he says. He seems as if he is fixing something, making something right. This is the way he is with a flat tire on a bike, she thinks, with a leaking pipe or a stuck window. The way he completely clears the large teak table, the table now too big for this small family, he moves in straight lines like a man with purpose, one who has made a decision, has a plan.

She sits in her chair, not sure where she belongs in this demonstration. "Here," he says, sitting down and pulling his chair close to hers, his shirt sleeves rolled over his forearms. He begins drawing. A circle, some spokes, some squares. "These are what genes look like," he begins, "like beads in jewelry."

She watches his hand, his voice getting steady and flowing with words she has heard but does not know. The diagram growing difficult with the explanation, larger and complicated, circles and arrows, chains... "Gene transplantation is now a reality..." more connections, more examples. "Ability to transfer genetic material from one cell to another of an entirely different species will permit biochemists like me to broaden our understanding of how cells—cancer cells, for example, reproduce..." More pencil lines emphasizing... As she watches him, his concentration, his small precise movements, she thinks he might be an insect, one magnified several hundred times, one that is hard at its work. "... And if

I take this one out what do you suppose will happen?" This is a question he is asking her, she realizes, and he has stopped talking and is listening, listening for the answer. She looks at the sheet of white paper, now covered with lines and circles, connections and separations. DNA... she thinks, *what is the question?* She is tired, suddenly more tired than she has felt in a long time, tired all over.

Her father looks at the top of her head, waiting. She cannot think of a single thing to say.

He looks at the diagram of genetic structure. What is he asking? Who is this girl sitting next to him, this stranger like a small animal almost, with her stranger's voice? Was her mother ever such a stranger? Is there any part of her that is not something strange and what does her silence say? What has he done? Looking at his pencil sketch, the odd structure of his science, his voice low and hollow, "Too much for ninth grade," he says. He holds his complicated drawing in front of him. "Different languages." He laughs at himself.

"It's complicated," she says, but she does not look at him. "Science is not my best subject." She seems to apologize. The two sit still in the awkward silence. "You tired?" he asks her in his voice for telling jokes, getting out of his chair suddenly. "Don't forget lunch money," he says, still in the joke voice, moving toward the sink to start on the dishes. Aki walks toward the dark empty part of the house, the noises of her father's housekeeping growing distant.

In her room she thinks of something she learned—a fact: one she might have forgotten if she did not regularly remind herself— water always goes down the drain clockwise in the Northern Hemisphere, Jupiter is the largest planet, Alaska is the largest state, China is the biggest country. One from today, what her father said, and she can remember: "Mutations can go on to reproduce themselves in normal ways."

Aki started the reminding game after her mother's death. She wanted to keep herself straight. The first thing she can remember thinking after her father came home from the hospital that day was: *The sun is rising now on some part of this planet.* Then, *Time starts in England, today is yesterday in India, today is yesterday there, today is yesterday somewhere.*...Keeping it all straight.

A couple of weeks later, it is her grandmother's birthday and the family will gather at the ranch: aunts, uncles, cousins. When

Aki and her mother would go to the ranch, they would always soak in the tub. They were always quiet then, in the tub, just the heat of the water and the wood and barn smells—leather, hay, earth. She can clearly remember her mother's face: the smooth line of her nose, her wide-set eyes, something funny she did to smile, how tiny her eyes got then, almost disappearing in the smile. Aki thinks of this while getting dressed for the party. When she gets to the kitchen her father has a pan covered with foil set on the table.

"What's that?" she asks.

"Peanut chicken—we always bring something," he says.

"You made it?" she asks.

"Stop 'n Shop," he says. "I stopped on the way home. I put it in our pan so it doesn't look store-bought."

"Good idea," she says, about the pan he thinks.

At Bachan's house, Aki is not sure where she belongs. The men always gather in one room, the women, tending to the meal and taking care of things, usually gather in another. This is the first time she has come without her mother, with just her father, and when they walk into the kitchen and are greeted, after a few moments with the women, her father leaves the women to their spooning and plate filling. He moves off to the room where the men sit, the TV playing a football game in the background. She stops, leans against a wall to watch the women. It is warm in the kitchen, full of movement and talk, full of flavor—chicken and fruit sauce, orange oil, sweet garlic, the sting of vinegar: the smell of her mother's cooking is there, in her grandmother's kitchen. "What is it?" she asks her grandmother. "I haven't smelled that in a long time."

"*Narai*," her grandmother shrugs, "a habit," motioning with her arm toward the table filled with dishes: rice spiced with bright, hot red ginger, sweet peas, pans of warm meats, vegetables, sashimi in thick tender rectangles. She finds a chair near the doorway in the room with the women, but where she can hear the men and where she can see her father's profile as he sits on the couch near a lamp.

"Who made the peanut chicken?" her grandmother asks, lifting the foil at the edge of the pan and peeking in, all the aunts stopping and listening for the answer.

"Daddy," she says. The women nod, looking at each other as if in agreement.

She looks at her father in the other room. The face he has is orange in the lamp light. Aki can hear the story he is telling about internment camp, Uncle Kei and a fifty-pound bag of potatoes Uncle Kei "found after it had fallen from a truck." She notices the ring in his words, "found after it had fallen from a truck." It is a voice he has for stories, she thinks. He laughs. "Three Japanese kids and fifty pounds of potatoes!" He laughs. "We traded it for ten pounds of rice. Thought we got a great deal, too!" He laughs again, a laugh she has not seen in many, many months, maybe has never seen: his head thrown back and his mouth in a wide surprise, his voice in clear resonance. A laugh that seems to last a long time.

She watches as he leans into a conversation. What is it he resembles there, like that? She cannot see, from her vantage point, whom he watches, nor hear, clearly, the voice he listens to. It does not matter.

She could learn cooking, she thinks, the combination of flavors in the air familiar, almost like a song she would recognize from just a few notes. Watching her father as he remembers his life, there in the orange light of her grandmother's lamp, as he knows to look over and see her watching him, to give her a small grin, then turns back to his talk, he appears a faraway planet, luminous and distant, one that will take study.

Kathryn Burak is a lecturer at Boston University and has fiction forthcoming in *Seventeen, Fiction, Epiphany,* and elsewhere.

THE PHENOMENOLOGY OF SHAME
/ Lynne Butler Oaks

WHEN SHE PASSES YOU in the hall, try to meet her eyes. Look away. Watch her smooth progress reflected in the window. She has not looked at you either. You notice her bruise-colored shoes. The soft soles. How thin her ankles are.

Back at the surgery station, pretend to ignore the whispers. Check charts. Note alterations of the vital signs. Don't participate by asking questions. You will learn enough to make a rough sketch of the facts.

They say it involved violence.

They say he may work here.

You read the note from the chief of staff asking night nurses to take alternate routes home. To park under streetlights.

It has happened before. They think it will happen again.

Later, you will learn the man has a signature, like a cologne; a tag line, like an advertisement. It is this: when he finishes, he takes the woman's panties out of her mouth, leans down very close to her face and says: Remember who you were and what you stood for.

This disturbs you. More than the bruises. More than the image of a window sliced in a perfect circle so as not to cut the arm that reaches in to find the lock. This makes you think he was raised like you: in a close family with a mother who loved him.

Refuse to comprehend. When the hospital's do-gooder tells you to be careful, be brittle. Say: If God was a gal, women wouldn't leak and breasts would be optional.

What you really want to say is: There are a finite number of evil acts in the universe and my odds have just improved.

The do-gooder will be a nutritionist, or a social worker. She will look at you as if your thoughts have spoken themselves. As if she wants to slap your face.

There are no alternate routes to your house. No deceptive curves or corners. Fasten your seatbelt and raise your consciousness about the activity in your rearview mirror. Think about the air in your tires, about how fragile they are. Grip the steering wheel. Test your braking reflexes.

Stop at the harshly lit 24-hour video store and rent enough black-and-whites to get you through till dawn. Choose Rita Hayworth, Greta Garbo, Tippi Hedren. Make them very old so the heroine can hold herself up on the hero's arm without shame. So that when he gets on the plane she can cry like her life is over.

Try to laugh at the way the women work their teeth over the long vowels. The way they snap their sentences like turtles. Imagine yourself through a brushed lens, soft and immaculate.

When it ends, use the sofa pillow to stifle your voice and cry with them: I need you. Don't leave me.

Take a kitchen knife with you into your bedroom. Examine its edge. Lie down and make a plan.

Think about buying a slingshot. Think about the possibility of victory at a distance.

The next day, during the patient care conference, you catch the do-gooder studying your face. Wonder if she's always been hostile to you. Decide the answer is yes. Two things could account for this.

One: she's a born-again and knows you're promiscuous.

Two: she's some kind of activist and thinks your feathered bangs and rose-colored blush are proof you have no sense of entitlement in the world.

Glare back. This will surprise her and she'll look away. Or it will intrigue her and she'll lower her eyelids. Smile.

Suspect the janitor who reads the trash and knows your maiden name.

The anesthesiologist looks at you across the ether screen and softly says: I think you desire me. The mask over his mouth makes his words seem isolated like tissue in a petrie dish. The speaker plays Schubert. The cellos are weeping.

You have just packed the baby's head in ice, frozen it to 15 degrees centigrade. You have stopped the blood. Now the surgeons can cut into her heart.

Say: I can meet you at the Motel 6 in the morning.

The anesthesiologist will pull his mask down and flash you a brilliant smile. Or he will stop looking at you altogether, monitor the monitors, ask you to bring him more whole blood. STAT.

Wait by the elevator, holding the transparent bags of blood above your waist. Notice the sign on the rosewood container: "Levels of radioactivity delivered to this box are small. There is no danger standing near this box." The sign has been crossed out with roller-coaster lines.

Become obsessed with reading things that have lines running through them. Scrape white-out off all the pages to see what they are keeping from you.

You trip over the threshold at the motel room. He says: I'm nervous too. He says: Show me yours and I'll show you mine.

You tell him you were nine the first time you saw one. You explain your parents were modest people who never left their bedrooms until they were fully dressed. You never even saw your father's bare feet. Then one day when you are walking home from violin lessons, a man calls you over to his car and asks you where the Safeway is. You look in and see him. You run home and tell your mother. She shakes your shoulders and says: Don't ever do that! Don't you ever do that! Then she calls the police. You hide under the bed the whole time the blue men are there, thinking about what it will be like, going to jail.

The anesthesiologist laughs at this last line. And he believes you when you say you can't come without your camisole on. This is precious to you. This is what you need. A man who finds the fruits of your repression exotic. Wish you could take this man home.

After, you share a cigarette, or a yogurt. He talks about his work. Which is pain, and sleep. He tells you some chronic people say they didn't know they were hurting until he stopped it.

The do-gooder has planned a retreat. She asks you to come. It is for "we women" who have been "affected by the incident."

She hands you a flyer and waits while you read it. It has a Title: Women of Courage: A Weekend for Survivors.

And a Place: Our Lady of the Mountains Retreat House.

There is a Facilitator. She is a "fully trained Christian feminist and survivor of sexual abuse."

And there is an Objective: To create sacred space where, together, we will affirm the spiritual dimensions of our journeys, minister to each other as a community of survivors through a variety of prayer forms, meditations, rituals for celebration, growth and healing.

Registration is limited to ten.

You say: I am not a victim.

She says: I am trained. I have a calling. You don't have to believe.

She says: Sometimes you have to let go. To let God.

Grip her arm. Raise your voice.

Say: God, lady, is a cancer in my heart.

She will blink. She will unclench your fingers. Very gently she will say: I hear you.

She hears you.

It has happened again. The do-gooder tells you this as you're walking away. She tells you this time the nurse won't be coming back. She says he broke her eardrum.

Wonder if the one it happened to heard his tag line. Wonder if the man, seeing how her ear bled, even bothered to say it.

Leave work early. Drive backwards down the one way. Put your tires over things that glint. Stop at the video store.

Slide the big knives out of the wooden block. Take the small steak and paring knives out of the drawer. Plant the knives in your yard, in a row leading to your door. Swords without soldiers.

Tips up, they catch the gleam of passing headlights. Use neon markers to make a sign: This Is Where I Live.

Slide in the first video. Push play. It is a horror movie. Decide they take too long on the exposition in these movies. They lie about the length of time the victims have to think. They lie about the light.

Stand in the background while the teenager's parents face the worst thing that will ever happen to them.

The oncologist explains what a bone marrow transplant is. They hear that enough chemicals will be put into their child's body to kill practically every blood cell—"that's how we get the bad ones"—and then at the last minute, new blood will be transplanted to rescue her.

The doctor asks them to sign the release. Hands them a pen. Waits.

When the parents recall this scene, after the girl dies, you will not be in the mental picture at all. But after the divorce, the husband will find he's not attracted to women with your hair color.

The girl begins giving the nurses fits. She refuses to play. She refuses to make the poodle with pink yarn and hangers. She has eaten its plastic eyes. She is threatening to pull out her IV.

The parents look at you. They are asking you to help. To stop her. The teenager is screaming. And bald. She looks like a Gerber baby with breasts. As she screams, she throws multicolored scarves into the air like Fall leaves.

Get these out of my room, she says.

But they are gifts, you say, as if it's only manners she's missing.

You are walking to your car. It is under the streetlight. You notice a sunflower caught in your license plate. Shadows behind your tires. You turn back to the hospital and call a cab.

The driver follows your instructions. Our Lady of the Mountains looks like a castle. The stones are gray. You touch the metal of the door handle. Your head begins to freeze. The driver picks up his receipt pad. The cold starts at your crown and moves forward to your temples.

Ice crystals are forming on your corneas.

Ask the cab driver to take you home. You understand this move for what it is: a failure of nerve. Redemption refused.

At home you brew decaf coffee and strain your ears for normal sounds. For sounds like those in the home you grew up in. The cape cod on a quarter acre. Who you were and what you stood for. Instead, you hear joists slipping. Ceilings decaying. No footsteps.

You slide in another video. Through the window you see the tips of the knives. They are turning white. Oxidized, maybe. Or covered with frost.

Lynne Butler Oaks's stories have appeared or are forthcoming in *Fiction International, Story Quarterly,* etc. *The Missouri Review* was the first to accept her fiction for publication.

AT A GLANCE / *Walter Bargen*

Beyond the front door a silhouette
on a low branch squawks, then flies,
as if only half-made for flight,
as though something medieval fell
from a lichen-stained parapet.

I guess wood duck, though
it is so far from steady water
I can't be sure, unlike the crows
who crowd the oaks nearly every morning,
clearing their harsh throats;

no doubt about their opaque presence.
It's the same with the wide-winged
glide of vultures in summer, blackened
by the sun, their raw heads cocking
loudly to one side as they pass

overhead; or last night, in a record
low April cold, as she held a flashlight and called, hearing a tear
in the forest floor, an explosion
of leaves and a stuttering squeal,

and directing the thin beam
like a baton, conducting the dark
from tree to tree and through the bushes
in between, searching for something
to save. As if life isn't teased

into death, slowly she approached
the cat, calmly calling its name,
picking it up and placing it over
her shoulder as she would a child
out too late and now safe. She turned

toward the house, the flashlight pointing
down, catching one at a time the brilliance
of her bare legs, a corner of her naked
hip, and the secret shining wing
flying up between her thighs.

REPORTING IN THE OFF SEASON
/ *Walter Bargen*

We are caught in the middle and Friday nights,
if the diamond is dry, the batter stands
at the plate, swings at some indefinable in between,
Zeno's sandlot gully where the ball is lost,

and watching the hypnotic stitching spinning
slowly, a celestial body knuckled through
space, the hidden speed, the umpire's explosive
report as the bat sweeps the air, a white

cane, and having touched nothing solid,
he is spun around, left on his knees
in a small swirl of dust, flood lights,
and deluge of jeers, and refusing for once

the shame, steps back, treading the finely
raked earth, and with the bat hits the side
of each raised shoe, loosening the clods
between the cleats; and maybe, every

Saturday morning thirty years ago, that is
what the Scrub Dutch thought washing south
St. Louis sidewalks, shoes off at the door,
worshippers of the perfect Nazi body,

cleanliness the way to connect, the soul's
home run, the everlasting Jesus floater
that catches the wind and clears the fence,
never falling on the warning track,

converting the terminal into the manageable;
and even now, in the off season, when the pencil-
thin stalks of golden rod are pedestals
for seamless balls of snow along the ridge

I follow, my shadow thrown on the far hillside,
slides over the steep slope, steals from trunk
to trunk, pennant material, but heading for someone else's house, sick of extremes and not sure

what to practice, one week below zero, the next
feeling warm as a summer evening, though it's hardly
above forty, and after a northerly's wide swing
snow is swept into a shining distance.

WALKING ON AIR / *Walter Bargen*

Blocks away and three o'clock in the morning,
the streets barricaded, and the high-rise
hotel burdened by too many stories

of satin, chauffeurs, and floodlights,
and the entropy of burlap, butts, and turned
tricks, both beginning and end carefully dynamited,

and for a moment, after the detonation,
windows trembled with a falling excitement,
and walls of concrete and brick stood on dust.

What brought us to watch precisely
when the brown cloud swelled
hundreds of feet into the air and rushed

through the streets, dirt swallowing
the windowed canyons between buildings,
and the jaundiced streetlights hardly reaching

us? I think we had tried all evening, our hands
kneading soft the masonry of each other's bodies,
but the walls were not ravaged so exactingly,

and still the room stood oddly open, as doubt
built its own thick-walled house, and we contrived
to watch the blur settle, leaving a film on sill

and glass that from the inside our fingers
could not reach to write the necessary words,
and the thin grimy ridges of accumulation

began to avalanche in dry tears as we tapped
the pane, as if on the eleventh floor we were
trying to attract someone's passing attention.

TRANSMISSIONS / *Walter Bargen*

The medals and euphoria of WWII
fading into night sweats and silence,
suburbs spreading across 1947,
house stacked against house,
it was Edward R. Murrow, the newscaster,
whose voice once choked with the sands
of Tobruk, rushed ashore on Normandy
and Omaha beachheads, followed V-1
rockets down into the London night,
who sat in a stateside television studio
watching the simultaneous live broadcasts
of the Pacific and Atlantic Ocean shores,
feeling he had stepped beyond man,
the first to inhabit all sides
of a continent at once, and not a single
stranded horseshoe crab to toss back
into the waves, or rank odor of kelp
rising with the noon heat;
to be everywhere and nowhere,
disembodied, a broadcasting angel.

Years later, after the liquor store
hold-up, the robber barricaded
in a rundown house in Linden,
New Jersey, surrounded by police,
took the time to answer the telephone
on the endtable beside the couch
in a stranger's house, and agreed
to be interviewed by a newspaper
reporter while the SWAT team broke
down the front door, targeting
their assault rifles at the figure
bent over the receiver, who said
to the flak-jacketed officers,
"Wait till I'm done," his voice
leaving his body across the wires.

BIRDING IN COSTA RICA / *Walter Bargen*

I struggle watching the tropics
slide across the screen
as easy as an oil sheen draining
across a rainy parking lot.
Not one airport appears,
not one alloy wing pointing
over a cloud-bound floor
or a patchwork of smoldering
slash and burn, only a map
with deep creases and the blurred
shadow of a finger held in front
of the lens saying here and here,
and when we find ourselves beside
two horse-mounted policemen,
their tunics rich as the petals
of bougainvillea on guard
in front of the opera house
built during the coffee boom
and closed after last year's
earthquake, I can almost smell
the diesel exhaust of a passing
pastel painted bus.

But outside the city
is where they strut and fly,
names exotic and common,
some arriving from the north,
others never doubting their vertiginous
greens. So much rises to join
their iridescent flights
and cluttered callings: termite
nests and leaf cutter ants,
howler monkeys and epiphytic cactus,
living among the branches,
as if declaring a higher ground,
furrowed with wind, a garden of air,

where an eternity roots
and all else soon falls away;

and though still found in one corner
of Monteverde, the resplendent
quetzal is more often seen in glyphs
of Montezuma's headdress
and the hummingbird as emblem
of his warrior's society
though they are all buried
in an empire of ruins,
and slaves' hearts remembered for the way
they contracted in priests' raised
hands though there's nothing left
now and even the Jesus Christ
lizard standing on its hind legs,
its neck stretched into a scaly sail,
running across the water
is oppressed by reflections
and dreams of sinking into feathers,
as we do, viewing the essence of flight,
the distillation of our days.

ZENO'S CINEMA / *Walter Bargen*

What I want is simple,
a camera clamped to a tripod
in a room where it cannot
be moved, set near a wall
and turned toward the opposite
one, which would be blank
and painted a stark gray,
a diagonal crack running
from floor to ceiling,
and at the same hour of the day,
everyday, under floodlights
angled from the corners,
the same child sitting in front
of the lens, back against
the wall, not expecting
or wanting anything too cute,
but three hundred and sixty-five days
for all the years, and the photographic
record mounted in albums,
or along the wall behind the camera,
or in front as if watching an echo
growing young, and maybe then,
the darkening hair, the cheekbones
and eyebrow's deepening, the perplexed
and vanishing smile, the hardening
chin, and the shadow of breasts
on a blouse, each photo a proof
we can stop and begin again.

Walter Bargen is the author of *Fields of Thenar, Mysteries in the Public Domain,* and *Yet Other Waters.*

PAST USELESS / *Nanci Kincaid*

AFTER THE NIGHT the sheriff came and got old Alfonso it was like he vanished from earth. Melvina didn't seem like she missed him, and never mentioned his name except when me and Roy said, "Tell us about the time old Alfonso got after you with that knife, Melvina. Tell us about him busting the door down with the axe. Tell about when he tried to choke you with a piece of clothesline. Tell about when ya'll tied him to that chair in the yard. Tell...."

"Men are past useless," Melvina said.

Mother said Melvina knows this because it's been proved to her over and over again. Now Alfonso Junior, her oldest boy, took over where his Daddy left off—proving it.

Alfonso Junior was sixteen and going through changes. More than wanting to be left alone—like he always did—but now going off who knows where and staying gone half the night. Then all the night. Won't say a word about it. As closed mouthed as he could be. So Melvina started guessing, and she guessed good. Alfonso Junior had found a girl.

It was Melvina's second boy, Skippy, who told her which girl, and Melvina went crazy, acting like Alfonso Junior had picked out the worst girl that could be picked. Virginia somebody. We never knew her last name but we'd seen her before because she used to come to Melvina's yard and hang around with Melvina's oldest girl, Annie. They plaited each other's hair, keeping an eye on the little children, sometimes drinking a Coca-Cola, or we'd see them hop-skipping up the dirt road going to the Snack Shack with a quarter. That was then. But this was now, Melvina throwing a fit over Alfonso Junior getting friendly with Virginia. "That fast girl shaking herself around this neighborhood, shaking herself in a boy's face," she said.

"I think it's sweet," Mother told Melvina, "Alfonso Junior's first love. It's puppy love."

"Puppy love my hind foot," Melvina fussed. "Ain't no puppy to it. It's pussy that boy's after. Ought to call it pussy-love, because ain't no puppy to it."

"Guess it wasn't anything to do with love back when old Alfonso got after you either, was it?" Mother said.

"I never was nothing like that fast girl. I didn't run up and down the street," Melvina said. "No sense in advertising—unless you got something to sell."

"Shoot," Mother said.

When me and Roy were in the yard we'd see Alfonso Junior sitting at the edge of the woods smoking a cigarette which was the other new thing he took up—smoking. We'd sneak close by him singing, *"Alfonso Junior and Virginia sitting in a tree, K-I-S-S-I-N-G, first comes love, then comes marriage, then comes Alfonso Junior with a baby carriage."* We sang loud and waited for Alfonso Junior to chunk a rock at us. He sat there sucking on that cigarette like he was half-asleep. Like Virginia-no-name herself could cause him to rise up out of that particular spot.

Me and Roy were used to being ignored by Alfonso Junior because since the day we moved in next door he had acted like we were invisible—except for the time he threw a fish head at us, or once that scoop of rabbit guts. Twice he had called me yellow head. "Get away from here, Yellow Head," he said, "or I'll take this snake out of my pocket and set it loose in your hair." Roy laughed his head off, so afterwards Alfonso Junior wasn't nearly as mean to him. Being treated bad by Alfonso Junior wasn't new to us, but it WAS to Skippy.

Suddenly Alfonso Junior didn't want anything to do with his own brother anymore—Skippy—who had shadowed him through every step of his life. "What's the matter with you?" Skippy asked him.

"I stopped being a jack-ass," he said. "You still at it."

To get even for the rejection, Skippy became Melvina's spy. It was his job to keep an eye on Alfonso Junior, trail him, report back to his mama and Skippy was good at it. He made a joke of it, how lovesick Alfonso Junior was, carrying on over Virginia, the loud-mouthed girl who used to hang upside down by her knees on a low limb letting her panties show and eating blackberries until her teeth were purple.

Since Melvina spent most of her life in our kitchen, me and Mother and Roy listened to the reports too. We knew everything about it. How Alfonso Junior scratched on Virginia's window, Virginia climbed out, and they went around some, no place much, up the road, the edge of the woods. Couldn't go far because Virginia had to listen for her brothers and sisters. Her Mama off strutting and Virginia staying home being the other Mama. Shouting distance was all. One holler away from the house.

Then it changed. Virginia climbed out the window, Alfonso Junior waited for her, his hat on his head, and they walked to the Snack Shack, that for-colored-only-cause-everything-costs-twice-as-much, gather-up-here-and-do-nothing store. They got them a cold drink and each a pack of salted peanuts because some way Alfonso Junior had started to have spending money. Cigarettes in his shirt pocket. Now Virginia and Alfonso Junior hung around the Snack Shack with the rest of the hanging-around people.

"Alfonso Junior been telling lies," Skippy told Melvina, as he sat at our kitchen table eating a sandwich Melvina made him out of our leftover breakfast bacon. "He's talking about all the money he's got and gon get more," Skippy said. "Said before long he's gon have a car—take Virginia for a ride when he gets it, let her wave to people out the window."

"Ahhhhhh," Mother smiled. "Alfonso Junior is dreaming big. Love makes you do that."

Melvina looked at Mother like she would like to slap her across the world.

Mostly Virginia ran around barefoot like everybody. Lots of nights we saw her walking up the sand-dirt roads late, stepping on sandspurs, flipping up the bottom of her foot so Alfonso Junior could pick the sandspur out. Took him a long time to do it, standing there holding her naked foot. In the moonlight. Virginia in her shorts or sometimes her little sack dress and her tender bare feet.

Once, late, when Walter drove by the Snack Shack we saw Virginia sitting out front when every nice girl was home in bed. Walter said, "What you guess she's up to—besides no good?" Just Virginia and Alfonso Junior sitting side by side on a bench in front of that closed store, Virginia drawing circles, Xs and swirls in the sand with her toe like it was a finger. Like her hands, sitting flat on the bench beside her were gone to sleep so her feet took over, and she drew with her toes. Erased with the soles of her feet. Big talking Alfonso Junior serious watching her do it.

Walter slowed down at the corner so me and Roy had time to yell out the window, "We see ya'll lovebirds," but we knew it was useless. You could look at them and see it. Walter could've driven the car right up to them with the lights and horn both blaring and they wouldn't have noticed.

But Alfonso Junior did notice FBI Skippy, his Mama's spy. He spotted him a hundred times and hollered, "You better not follow me around. You might learn something you too young to know."

Then Virginia laughed and Skippy slung a rock at both of them and came home to tell it. "Fools," he said. "Kissy-lipped, body-rubbing fools."

The next thing was Alfonso Junior had more than a pocketful of spending change. Not like when he took empty bottles to the Snack Shack for deposit pennies, or when he mowed an old woman's grass, or painted her porch, or climbed on her roof to clean the pine straw off. This was real money. Regular. Like a job. "I seen Alfonso Junior with a roll of money as big as his fist," Skippy told Melvina.

But when Melvina asked Alfonso Junior where he got it, he said, "Mama, you're crazy and your feet ain't mates."

So Melvina quit asking. When Alfonso Junior slipped a five into her apron pocket, or left ten in an empty coffee cup, or twenty that time in her shoe so when she slipped her foot into it she felt a lump, pulled out a wad of bills and counted up twenty dollars, she didn't say, "Where in the world did you get this?" She just put the money to good use, didn't ask questions she might hate to hear the answer to.

Then Skippy tells Melvina that Alfonso Junior and Virginia quit bothering with the Snack Shack, which all it was was a gas station anyway. Now Virginia put on shoes and fixed herself up with red lips and she and Alfonso Junior walked all the way up to the Blue Bird Cafe, smoking cigarettes, Alfonso Junior whispering "honey, you look good" to Virginia. Couldn't take his eyes off her, or his hands.

"Them two kids think because they're lovesick, it means they're grown," Melvina said.

I pictured them dancing in the Blue Bird Cafe, that dark, pump-house, hot-box with the blue chicken on the sign, a cinderblock square squirming, throbbing. Music pouring out of it, slow and easy—like something leaking, supposed to stay inside, but oozing out, easy. And the people all jittering, rumbling and slow bouncing on rubber legs. Red-lipped Virginia by Alfonso Junior's side dancing with her shoes on. People saying, "Hey, Alfonso Junior, where's your Daddy?" because everybody in French Town knew old Alfonso before he disappeared—the king of the Blue Bird Cafe. Now Alfonso Junior was his Daddy's just-like-him-good-time son.

It was Walter who found out Alfonso Junior was running whiskey. Taking some to somebody's house, some out to the car waiting in the street. Walter said he'd seen Alfonso Junior carry liquor so a police with his dog walked right past him, nodded, and never knew for one second the boy was carrying liquor. "Ya'll making something out of nothing," Walter said. "Myself, I like to see a enterprising nigger."

Walter knew this because it wasn't unheard of for him to come home with a bottle of whiskey in the glove compartment of his truck. Nobody mentioned it because Mother was against liquor. She voted every time to keep Leon County dry. "Ain't nobody bootleggers love any better than Christian women," Walter said. He thinks it's handy, Alfonso Junior running whiskey right next door—a young boy like him.

It worried Melvina sick. "Lord, Melvina, let the boy be," Walter said. But she kept sending Skippy evening after evening and he kept bringing her reports which Mother and us stayed in on the best we could. Skippy was dedicated.

One night he tiptoed around, looking at the Blue Bird people like they were in a picture show and he's paid money to watch them. Skippy in the bushes. Skippy behind a car. Skippy peeping in the door the way a mouse peeps in a cathole. Alfonso Junior, who was minding his own business, saw him, and shouted, "I don't need none of this hide-and-seek tattletaling." He chased Skippy until he caught him, then beat what Walter called *the living hell* out of him.

It was the only time I ever saw Skippy cry. He hobbled down to our house looking for Melvina. Nine o'clock at night and Mother and Melvina in the kitchen trying to Rit dye a bedspread in the sink, heating pots of hot blue water on the stove. Melvina was beside herself at the sight of Skippy, his mouth pouring blood. "Merciful God," she said, grabbing a rag, dipping it in the dye water, pressing it to his lip.

"Walter!" Mother yelled. "Walter!"

He hurried to the kitchen. "Boy, you look like you walked into an airplane propeller," he said.

Skippy was torn to pieces. Mother sat him in a kitchen chair and he went limp. Then Melvina held him while Mother poured rubbing alcohol on his busted lip. He jerked and Mother kept blowing on it like she was puffing out candles on a cake. "He might need stitches," she said.

"I ain't getting stitches," Skippy snarled, yanking away from Mother and Melvina, tears going down his face, one eye swollen closed and his lip puffed.

"Good Lord," Walter said, standing with the newspaper in his hand. "Ya'll let the boy alone." Before Mother and Melvina could say anything Skippy was out the door.

The next day Alfonso Junior was crazy enough to come straggling home and Melvina threw a Melvina-style fit that could scare somebody who wasn't used to it. He was barely in the yard when Roy yelled, "Alfonso Junior, you in trouble."

Melvina tore out of our kitchen after him, so did I, and Mother came. We gathered up, all of us, at the edge of Melvina's yard and she started right in with laying-down-the-law, thou-shalt-thou-shalt-not, too-big-for-your-britches stuff. Hollering at Alfonso Junior, mad, waving her arms like she did when Nappy got into the poison roach pellets that time or when one of her little boys tore the screen out of the door by laying on the floor banging his feet up against it until he had it all the way ripped out, just did it for no reason. Throwing a fit now like she did then because it's the only thing a person can do in some circumstances. Melvina saying, "Beat your brother like that, like a dog."

Now Alfonso Junior was mad too. Wanted Melvina to quit yelling and she wouldn't do it. "You gon run me off like you run off your own husband if you don't shut up."

"Don't be saying run-off-your-husband to me."

"Run Daddy right out of her into another lady's house. Just stayed on his back until he's gone. Found him a woman that knows how to treat somebody without wagging her tongue all the time."

"You crazy talking."

"Ain't crazy," Alfonso Junior said. "Daddy ain't gone. He's up in French Town, at the Blue Bird every night. He's been up there. Ain't dead or in jail or nothing else. Just gone from your mouth flapping breeze."

"Don't lie to me," Melvina screamed, looking at her no-count son she'd been worrying herself sick over, and now him acting just as useless as his Daddy that he says is not gone.

"I ain't lying," Alfonso Junior said.

"If you're not—then you're crazy."

"I seen him myself," Alfonso Junior said. "He's staying up in French Town with his new woman. Name's Rose Lee. Seen both of them. He's in Tallahassee same as the rest of us."

Now, even though Alfonso Junior is a liar, we believed him anyway because it was such hateful news and he was enjoying it like it was the truth. Me and Roy and Mother believed everything colored people said because they shocked us into it, but Walter was the kind that didn't believe none of it. If he'd been listening to Alfonso Junior he'd have said, "Hogwash," and gone back in the house where the fan was going. But us, everything sounded like the truth to us, so we believed it. The news went over us like a bucket of water.

Melvina was like Walter, not quick to believe. Her way was to never believe anything—at first. She stood with hands on her hips, elbows jutted out like flaps on a boat, for balance, or like brakes. She was a woman who dared the truth to get itself believed.

Melvina took the news of old Alfonso being alive the way people usually took the news of somebody being dead. "He's no such a thing," she said.

"Is too, Mama."

"Then say you swear and hope to die."

"I ain't saying hope to die. I'm saying I seen Daddy."

"And him with a woman?"

"Yes."

"What kind of woman?"

"A woman woman. Some woman probably don't boss him day to night."

"Named Rose?"

"Rose Lee."

"How do you know her name?"

"Somebody said here come old Alfonso and Rose Lee. And here they come, so I know it."

"Your Daddy's back?"

"Been back."

Melvina got a look, like her face was a tire going flat, a retread losing its patch. The rest of us stood staring at her, our own memories of old Alfonso leaping up like ghosts from a grave. Old Alfonso was not dead. Not gone forever. It was like if they told you the war was over and then later you found out it was a trick—you looked up and saw bombs falling out of the sky and you knew it was a trick. Maybe old Alfonso would come back and take up where he left off—trying to kill Melvina every day of her life.

Alfonso Junior struck a match, put it to his cigarette, then held it in his hand until it burned down to his fingertips. He smiled letting his teeth show.

"You ought to be ashamed," Mother said.

"Can't apologize for the truth," Alfonso Junior said.

"Of course you can," Mother said.

Alfonso Junior turned away, "Got a woman waiting." He strutted across the yard toward the dirt road.

Me and Roy and Mother circled around Melvina like sticks propping up a leaning thing and watched Alfonso Junior walk away until he was completely out of sight. Melvina knew, same as we did, that she couldn't say one thing to him, not that he would listen to, not when he had more spending money rattling in his pocket than she had to her name. Not since he was his Daddy's boy—his Daddy highstepping with some woman named a flower—and Melvina just somebody both of them think they don't need anymore.

"Are you scared, Melvina?" Roy said.

"Is old Alfonso coming back?" I said.

"Don't worry, Melvina," Mother said, "if he does, Walter will be waiting with his gun." Melvina was stone quiet.

Afterwards the rest of us tried not to think too much about old Alfonso being back. We kept our fears private. I only thought about him when it got dark. I knew he could hide in the dark, matched it perfect, blended right in, and so it seemed he was everywhere at night, watching me, getting ready to climb in the window, slit my throat and set the house on fire. But I only thought about it when I was in bed with the door closed. I didn't dwell on it.

But Melvina did. Old Alfonso being back was strong on her mind. Sometimes she looked out the window thinking he might be walking down the road, like she was expecting him to come calling, or to come home carrying his clothes in a cardboard suitcase, like she was expecting him to do something, but she didn't know what. Just expecting him.

"Melvina, it's a blessing him having some other woman to make miserable instead of you," Mother said.

"Maybe he's a useless man," she said, "but he's MY useless man."

It didn't make sense, Melvina suddenly claiming old Alfonso, calling him hers and saying she's got papers to prove it. It was a colored people thing—the way they counted people same as other people counted acres or money in the bank. If Walter said, "I got a Ford pick-up and a used Chevrolet needs work," Melvina'd say, "I got all them boys, Annie, and a no-count husband somewhere." If Granddaddy said, "I got eighty-eight acres out in Macon County, Alabama," Melvina'd say, "So what? I got a house full of kids and one husband too, belongs to me legal."

She acted like she forgot that time old Alfonso knocked her tooth out, or when he sliced her across the chest where she's got that pink scar. So I said, "Melvina, what you want with a man like old Alfonso? He nearly killed you once a week."

"He didn't start out that way, baby," Melvina said. "Used to be old Alfonso'd be singing when the rest of the world was mad about something. He wouldn't hurt nobody or nothing back then."

She thinks I'm crazy enough to believe it.

Melvina was sitting on the sofa with a sack of pecans in her lap, and a nutcracker in her hand, shelling the pecans Granddaddy brought us to make pies with at Thanksgiving. The pecans reminded me of little skulls, Melvina popping them open with a loud cracking noise, sometimes pausing to eat the brains out of one of them.

Mother was lining up the LIFE magazines in a fan shape on the coffee table, arranging them by date. "One thing I know and I learned it hard," she said, "is you can't change a man, Melvina." She began making a second fan out of the TIME magazines, arranging them the same way. "But it's a woman's natural instinct to try."

Melvina shook her head knowingly, "It's a curse goes all the way back to Eve."

"I'm not saying not to try to change old Alfonso, Melvina— spend your whole life trying if you want to—just as long as you know it never will do any good."

"I'm going to pray about it," Melvina said.

"You might as well," Mother said, "because it takes God in heaven to change a man."

A couple of weeks later as Melvina stepped out our kitchen door to walk home after work, screaming and shouting erupted up at her house. Roy and me heard it and tore outside past Mother who hollered, "You two stay in this house!" Then she ran after us, but stopped beside Melvina on the back steps. "What in the world is wrong?" she said.

Next door we saw Annie dash out of Melvina's house carrying Nappy, the baby, with her. "Stop that," she screamed. "Alfonso Junior, stop!" Her voice was a knife slashing into a perfectly harmless afternoon.

Skippy ran to Melvina's yard just as Alfonso Junior chased Virginia out of the house onto the porch. Virginia tried to get away, but Alfonso Junior grabbed her, and before she could get loose, swung at her, trying to slap her face, but he missed and she crumpled down on the porch, screaming. He let go of her, and she fell sideways hitting her head against a metal chair. She let out a bloody murder wail.

Annie and Skippy could not get to her because if they came close Alfonso Junior kicked at them. "Let her alone," he hollered. "I'm just making her understand something."

"Her nose is bleeding. Looks like her nose is broke," Annie hollered.

Virginia was howling like a cat. Every time she tried to get up Alfonso Junior shoved her back down. Annie screamed for him to stop. Melvina's dogs were barking.

"Do something, Melvina," Mother said. "You got to make him quit it."

"You the one calls it puppy love," Melvina said. "You the one says it's *sweet.*" Melvina, who knew everything about men, folded her arms across her chest, stood dead still, and watched the fight with a couple of glass eyes.

"Go back in the house!" Mother hollered to me and Roy, but we didn't do it.

Virginia was crying loud, but she didn't slap back or tear into Alfonso Junior like she ought to have. She didn't claw his eyes out, scratch his face, or call him filthy names. She only cried. Alfonso Junior couldn't make her stop for the longest time. The more he yelled the more she cried. The more he shoved her the less she resisted until she was lying flat and still on the porch and there was nothing else Alfonso Junior could do but stop. There was no further down he could push her so he just stood on the porch looking stupid and hitting his fist against the door frame.

"I hate you, Alfonso Junior," I yelled. "I hate your guts."

"Shut up," Roy said, slapping his hand over my mouth. "Are you crazy?"

Then, slowly, Virginia began to sit up straight-backed and stiff, making herself available to all the hitting Alfonso Junior could ever come up with, like if he was looking for a target, she would see to it he got a bull's-eye. But he didn't come up with any more hitting, he just looked at her with her hands over her face, her bloody nose, that shake-crying she was doing and he started this, "Baby, you okay?" mess and "Honey, I ain't meant to do it." He squatted down and hugged Virginia, like hugging a wooden plank, and put his face all around on hers getting blood everywhere, and on his shirt too.

Virginia was rock quiet, not moving except to try and wipe the blood away with the back of her hand. She stood up, slow,

Alfonso Junior helping her, but her like she didn't see Alfonso Junior whatsoever. As far as she was concerned the boy was invisible. When she began to walk, he bunched himself like a clumsy crutch beside her and leaned against her, but it was useless and he quit because, to Virginia, Alfonso Junior was as good as not there.

Annie was still fussing, saying, "Look what you done." Me and Roy stood at the edge of our yard, our toes on the line, pretending we were deaf when Mother said, "Did you hear me? I said come back here."

Virginia didn't say a word, not to Annie or anybody. She walked across the yard with her head held back like a queen, pinching the tip of her nose closed. Her perfect posture, the regal slant of her head, her eyes looking directly into the sun as she walked— the black inner tube of my heart, overpumped, was ready to burst with love and fury.

Alfonso Junior was like a puppy yapping at Virginia's heels. He could not be still. He could not be quiet. "Talk to me, baby," he said, circling her like a dog about to be fed, getting up under her feet so she couldn't go straight. Because he didn't have a tail to wag he wagged his arms. He stood in front of her like a roadblock but she didn't stop walking, so he walked backwards, his arms open, waving up and down, him saying, "Ain't no sense to get mad. I ain't meant nothing by it. Come on, baby, now."

Alfonso Junior was so ashamed that any minute I thought he would lay himself down flat across the road and let Virginia walk right over him if she wanted to, or he'd grab one of her feet, hold on, let her drag him all the way up California Street or all the way to Georgia. He wanted to kiss her but she wouldn't stop walking long enough. He was begging and prancing in circles like a dog after his own tail. He said, "I'm going to buy you something nice. You too sweet to be acting like this, baby."

It was a pitiful thing to watch. Anybody loving somebody that much. I could hardly stand to watch it. Alfonso Junior was all over the girl with sweet words. I wondered if Virginia was going to love him again tomorrow—or next year, or ever? I wondered if she would be like Melvina and keep on loving a man whose favorite thing was to almost kill her, over and over, and then be sorry afterwards. Maybe being sorry for something was the best feeling in the world and that's why Alfonso Junior liked it so much.

Run, Virginia! I wanted to scream. But I stood like the cat had got my tongue. I wanted to scream for Virginia to pull out seven guns and shoot Alfonso Junior for every day of the week, shoot him in all the places where his heart should be. Don't love him, Virginia, don't spend a minute of your life loving him. Me and Roy and Mother will help Melvina hold him down—the whole world will hold him down—and let you get even. Let you slap his face a thousand times, until he cries and says he's sorry.

As soon as Alfonso Junior and Virginia were out of sight up the road, then Melvina walked home, with Mother on the steps, yelling, "It scares me, Melvina, the way your boys take after their daddy."

Melvina walked past me and Roy. She looked at us with eyes as sharp as pins. "Scat," she said, waving her hand, shooing us off, disgusted. "Get away from my yard."

She thought we didn't feel things. I wanted to tear my skin open and show Melvina my beating heart. This world tied love into hateful knots and our lifetimes were too short to unravel them. She thought someone needed to slap some love into us so we could understand that. I think she wanted to do it herself—right then. "Go home," she ordered.

"We don't have to," Roy said. "It's a free country."

We ran home terrified by Melvina's laughter. It was louder than screaming. She slapped her hands together. Her closed eyes set loose a flood.

Nanci Kincaid has a collection of fiction due out next year. Other stories have appeared or are forthcoming in *Ontario Review, Southern Exposure*, and *The Crescent Review*.

The Best of
The Missouri Review
Fiction, 1978–1990

Edited by Speer Morgan, Greg Michalson, and Jo Sapp

"A marvelous, historic collection by some of the most compelling of contemporary literary talents."
—*Louise Erdrich*

"An important anthology from an important place: *The Missouri Review* has found the heart of American fiction"
—*Thomas McGuane*

"The Shakespeare Squadron is on the march! Bowles, Carver, Hempel, Shacochis, Mahfouz, and Ohle—the American Beckett—they're all here. The short story isn't dead after all. Read on!"
—*William Burroughs*

"*The Best of* THE MISSOURI REVIEW is a first-rate gathering, top of the line, and splendidly representative. It belongs on the shelves of everyone who cares about the art of the short story."
—*George Garrett*

Includes stories by:

Will Baker • Russell Banks • Stephanie Bobo
Paul Bowles • François Camoin • Ron Carlson
Raymond Carver • Alice Denham • Robb Forman Dew
Jim Hall • Amy Hempel • Wally Lamb • Kevin McIlvoy
Naguib Mahfouz • David Ohle • Ninotchka Rosca
Bob Shacochis • and many more!

March, 320 pages, $32.50 (cloth), $15.95 (paper)

University of Missouri Press——
2910 LeMone Boulevard • Columbia, MO 65201 • 800–828–1894

The Laurel Review

Some of our contributors:

A.R. Ammons
David Baker
Jim Barnes
Bruce Bennett
Wendy Bishop
Carol Bly
Frederick Buell
Kathryn Stripling
   Byer
Michael Carey
Henry Carlile
Jared Carter
Kelly Cherry
David Citino
Stephen Corey
Philip Dacey
Richard Duggin
Stephen Dunn
Charles Edward
   Eaton
Julie Fay

Gary Fincke
Donald Finkel
Stuart Friebert
Elton Glaser
Albert Goldbarth
William Hathaway
Michael Heffernan
Art Homer
Colette Inez
Richard Jackson
William Kloefkorn
Ted Kooser
Sydney Lea
Peter Makuck
Michael Martone
Walter McDonald
Erin McGraw
David McKain
Heather Ross Miller
Judith Moffett
Howard Nemerov

Sharon Olds
Carole Simmons
   Oles
Greg Pape
Paula Rankin
David Ray
Pattiann Rogers
CarolAnn Russell
Scott Russell Sanders
Reg Saner
Maurya Simon
Katherine Soniat
Marcia Southwick
William Stafford
George Starbuck
Mary Swander
Ann Townsend
Robert Wallace
Ronald Wallace
Don Welch
Robley Wilson, Jr.

SUBSCRIPTIONS: $8 per year, $14 for two years / Available back issues: $3.50 each / Make checks payable to: GreenTower Press / Department of English / Northwest Missouri State University / Maryville, MO 64468

Financial assistance for this project has been provided by the Missouri Arts Council, a State Agency

The Georgia Review

—— *Spring 1991* ——

> Frederick Busch's *The Rub*

> Robert Finch's *Being at Two with Nature*

> Thomas Gavin's *The Truth Beyond Facts: Journalism & Literature*

> Árpád Göncz's *Politics in Literature, Literature in Politics*

> Jane Hirshfield's *The World Is Large & Full of Noises: Thoughts on Translation*

> James Longenbach's *Why It Must Be Abstract*

FICTION by Phil Condon & Max Garland.

POETRY by Marvin Bell, Liz Brixius, Billy Collins, Lynn Emanuel, Starkey Flythe, Jr., Christine Gebhard, Debora Greger, Richard Hill, Debra Hines, Yusef Komunyakaa, Steve Kronen, Linda McCarriston, Peter Meinke, Michael Mott, Linda Pastan, Thomas Russell, David Swanger, & Tom Whalen.

GRAPHICS: *Paper Play* by Akiko Sugiyama.

BOOK REVIEWS by Madeline DeFrees, Gary Gildner, Judith Kitchen, Erin McGraw, Sanford Pinsker, Richard Watson, & others.